Luke into Jesus

How to Live as Children of His Kingdom

by Graeme C. Young

Table of Contents

As you read this book, you will see what I have found in exploring Luke's Gospel.

What you would not see, unless I mentioned it here, is that I have been able to give time to serving Jesus in projects like this because there are people who have supported my work over many years. This book is as much a result of their giving as it is of my writing. Perhaps, like me, you will want to say, "Thank you" to God for such friends and for their hidden help.

Graeme C. Young

graeme@youngresources.co.uk
www.youngresources.co.uk

Introduction

Welcome to
Luke into Jesus – how to live as children of His Kingdom

Luke into Jesus is a guide to understanding what is written about Jesus in the book in the Bible which is called Luke.

• Younger readers will find that the words used are simple and easy to understand.
• Readers who are new to studying the Bible will find clear explanations of things that they may not have learned about before.
• Older readers who know the stories well will find more for them to discover.
• Families or small groups who use this book as they read Luke together will find plenty to talk about.

The purpose of this guide is for us all to be ready for everything that Jesus wants us to be and to do as children of his Kingdom, whatever age we are.

There are many versions of the Bible, and in some places they use different words from each other. **Luke into Jesus** is written in a way that helps every reader to follow the notes, whatever version of the Bible they are using.

The New Testament was written first in Greek, and studying the words used in that language has helped to make clear some things that are not obvious in our English translations.

Reading the Bible is like going on a journey with Jesus. **Luke into Jesus** is a guide to help readers on that journey. It is only a guide. How we journey with Jesus depends on how we respond to what the Holy Spirit shows us as we read the Bible.

Luke into Jesus explores the book of Luke in 89 parts. Each part has notes about it in 4 sections:

INFORMING:
explaining things that will help us in understanding the passage.

INTRODUCING:
showing how the passage helps us to get to know Jesus better.

INSPIRING:
seeing how the Holy Spirit is at work in the passage and in Jesus.

INSTRUCTING:
discovering lessons we can put into practice in living for Jesus.

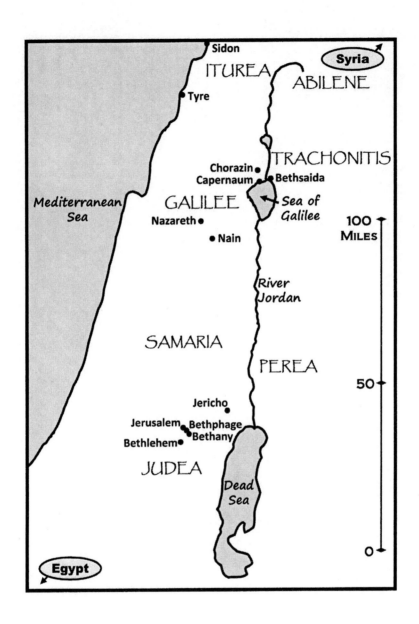

1. Luke 1v1-4 Luke introduces his book about Jesus

Informing:

• This book was written by Luke, a Christian doctor who was part of a team who travelled to different places to help people to get to know Jesus. He describes part of his own experience in Acts chapters 20 and 21. Luke was a friend of Paul who wrote other parts of the New Testament. Paul describes him as the loved doctor in Colossians 4v14.

• It was written to Theophilus. We do not know who he was, but the title "most excellent" shows that he had some position of importance as a leader. Theophilus is a good name as it means "God's friend", so if you want to be God's friend, this book was written for you!

• Special things have been happening. Luke has heard about these things from people who were there when they happened. Luke has put together his book of what happened to encourage us to be clear and sure about Jesus.

Introducing:

• This is a "Jesus Book", describing who he is, what he did and what he said. Every part of it introduces us to something more about him.

• Luke wrote two books, "Luke" and "Acts". At the beginning of his second book, "Acts", Luke says that in his first one he had written about all the things that Jesus had begun to do and to teach before he was taken up into heaven. It was what Jesus had <u>begun</u> to do because in "Acts", Jesus was still alive in heaven and was still doing things through Luke and the other Christians that Luke wrote about.

Inspiring:

• Luke says that it seemed good to him to write his account. It was actually a very special idea from the Holy Spirit. The Holy Spirit was inspiring (that word means breathing into) Luke in his writing, so that the words he wrote were not just what he wanted to say, but what God wanted to say through him.

• When we want others to get to know Jesus, the Holy Spirit will show us ways of helping them and will give us what we need so that we are able to do it.

Instructing:

• Other people had known and written about Jesus, but Luke wanted to find out for himself and to be used in helping others, so he gave his time to this study of Jesus' life. Now we are giving our time to reading Luke's book because we want to know Jesus better. This will help us to be ready to be used by God in helping others.

• Luke wrote the whole book to help one friend, and here we are reading it today! We never know how important the help we give to one friend might be in God's plans.

2. 1v5-10 Zechariah serves as the chosen priest

Informing:
• Here at the beginning of this chapter and in the first verses of the next two chapters, Luke says when these events took place. They are not made up stories; these things really happened.
• The temple was in Jerusalem. It was the special place where people came together to worship God. The priests all came from the same tribe – the Levites. They were divided into groups who took it in turns to come to the temple and to be on duty there for two separate weeks each year (as well as for the big festivals).
• From the group on duty, one priest each day was chosen by lot (that is like throwing dice to decide). He would then be the one to burn incense that day on the altar in the inner temple. Many of the priests were never chosen, and those who were chosen, were only allowed to do it once in their lifetime.

Introducing:
• In their worship, along with wanting to be close to God and to obey him, people were waiting for God to keep his promises about the coming of a special person, and someone who would prepare for that person's coming. In the last book of the Old Testament, written about 400 years before, the prophet Malachi had written (Malachi 3v1) that God was saying that his messenger would come, and that then the Lord whom they were looking for would come to his temple. At the beginning of this day in Jerusalem, it still looked as if nothing was happening.

Inspiring:
• God had noticed how Zechariah and Elizabeth had lived. Their big disappointment at not having children had not stopped them loving and serving God. The Holy Spirit can help us to keep trusting Jesus even when we face disappointments.
• Although everyone thought that Zechariah had been chosen that day "by chance", it was actually the Holy Spirit who was making things happen so that what took place would be what God had planned. Even the

"chance" happenings in our lives can be places where the Holy Spirit is at work.

Instructing:
• If we, like Zechariah and Elizabeth, are living our lives for God, then we can be sure that he is planning to use us in his purposes.

• Things begin to happen when we pray.

• We never know when the Holy Spirit might decide to use an ordinary day to do something extraordinary with is, so let us be ready every day.

3. 1v11-25 An angel speaks to Zechariah

Informing:
- An angel appears. Who are angels? They are heavenly beings so they are different from human beings. Gabriel said that he stood in the presence of God, so he had come from heaven.
- The word "angel" means "messenger", so when angels appear they are being God's messengers to the people they appear to.
- What do angels look like? We often think of angels as having wings, and some of them are described in that way in the Bible. Usually, however, when an angel is appearing to someone they are described as looking like a man, and this is how Gabriel is described when he appeared in the Old Testament to the prophet Daniel (Daniel 8v15-18). Sometimes it is clear that angels who appear are heavenly beings because they are shining brightly, at other times they look just like ordinary people.
- Elijah was an Old Testament prophet, someone who told people what God wanted to say to them.

Introducing:
- What is the most important thing in this surprise event? It is not the appearing of the angel, or the promised special baby, or the wonderful things he will do, or the special sign of Zechariah not being able to speak. The most special thing is what the words of the angel point to. If John was to get the Lord's people ready for him, that meant that the Lord (Jesus) was coming soon!
- What Jesus is about to do is always more important than anything else that is happening.

Inspiring:
- The Holy Spirit is at work on God's great plans, and also at work in a little baby.
- The Holy Spirit gave the words that are written in the Bible, so Malachi wrote (Malachi 4v5,6) of God's promise to send to them the prophet Elijah who would turn the hearts of the fathers to the children and the hearts of the children to their fathers. Now these words are said to apply to the

coming baby, John.

• John was to be filled with the Holy Spirit from before he was born, not just when he was grown up doing his special work. God wants us all to be filled with the Holy Spirit so that we are ready for whatever he has for us to do.

Instructing:

• Zechariah and Elizabeth had prayed for a child. Elizabeth felt ashamed that they had not had a child. God <u>had</u> heard their prayer, and he wanted to bring them lots of joy, but he held off from answering their prayer because he had a bigger and better plan in mind.

• God is committed to loving and blessing us. If things do not work out as we have hoped they will, God has a greater plan in mind that will make us really happy.

• God wants us to be ready to receive what he says, even when it sounds impossible.

• When we speak to God, we expect that he will hear us and do something. When God speaks to us, he expects that we will hear him and do something!

4. 1v26-38 An angel speaks to Mary

Informing:

• Although Mary has a very special place in God's plans we are told nothing about her life before this. We only know that she was a young woman who was going to marry Joseph. All we can discover about his life is that he was a carpenter and that he wanted to obey God's law. If this is all we are told, it is because this is what the Holy Spirit wants us to know.

• David was God's chosen king of Israel about 1000 years before this time.

• Jacob, who lived about 700 years before David, was promised many blessings by God. God changed Jacob's name to Israel.

Introducing:

• It is very clear from what is said here that Jesus was a unique baby; he did not have a human father. He comes as God's son, King of God's people and the one who saves people from their sins. "Jesus" means saviour – the one who saves.

• Mary was told by the angel to name the baby, Jesus. In Matthew's book we find what happened to Joseph. In a dream an angel told him about the baby and said that he should name him, Jesus. It must have been very special when Mary and Joseph told each other!

Inspiring:

• The Holy Spirit is the one who makes God's plans happen. The promise to Mary is quite like Jesus' promise to his followers in Luke's second book, where he says that they would receive power when the Holy Spirit came upon them. (Acts 1v8)

• The Holy Spirit, when received by Mary, brought Jesus into the world. The Holy Spirit, when received by us, can bring something of the presence and power of Jesus into the world through what we say and do.

Instructing:

• At this time Mary was shown what God wanted to do in her life. God has special plans for each of us which he will show us at the right time. We never need to be afraid of his plans.

• Mary is a good example for us: God shows her what he plans to do with her. She asks for the information which will help her to know what to do and what not to do.

She commits herself to serving God and trusts him to make it happen. From God comes the power to make happen whatever he has said.

• The angel encouraged Mary's faith by telling her about Elizabeth. What God has done in the lives of people we know should encourage us to believe for what he is going to do in our lives.

5. 1v39-45 Mary visits Elizabeth

Informing:
- When Mary came to visit, Elizabeth had been pregnant for about six months, so when Mary entered the house she would probably have seen by the shape of Elizabeth's body that what the angel had told her about Elizabeth was true. If not, it looks like before Mary had the chance to sit down she heard about Elizabeth's baby!
- There is no mention of any conversation with Zechariah, because, of course, he was still unable to speak.

Introducing:
- This is the first welcoming of Jesus into the world. Elizabeth recognises that there is a baby in Mary's womb, even though there would be no outward sign of this. She also speaks of Mary's baby as "my Lord". We do not know whether the Holy Spirit had shown her anything about this before she spoke, or whether it happened as she spoke, but either way, it was the Holy Spirit who told her of the presence of Jesus and of who he is.

Inspiring:
- This was a wonderful "Holy Spirit meeting". As soon as Mary says, "Hello", the unborn baby in Elizabeth (at not much more than 24 weeks) jumps at the presence of Jesus who is probably less than four weeks from the time of beginning to grow in Mary's womb. So, unborn children are special. From before they grow into the shape of a baby (at about 8 weeks) they are special persons, and unborn children are able to respond to the presence of Jesus and the Holy Spirit.
- The Holy Spirit filling Elizabeth gave her words of knowledge (knowing things that only God could have told her) and words of prophecy (a message from God), and it came in a shout. She cried out with a loud voice, not in ordinary conversation but with a Holy Spirit outburst.

Instructing:
- I think that this event was the happiest and most exciting thing that had happened until that point. Mary was so excited that she hurried

across the country to see Elizabeth. The Holy Spirit was so excited that as soon as Mary and Elizabeth met, things began to happen. The unborn baby, John was so excited that he jumped inside Elizabeth's womb. Elizabeth was happy because she believed that what God had spoken about would happen. Mary was happy because she believed that what God had spoken about would happen. The lesson for us is to believe what God has said to us, and to know the happiness and excitement of seeing his plans work out in our lives.

• God gave Mary and Elizabeth each other to share with. When not everyone understands or agrees with what God is doing with us, he will give us friends to share with who do know and accept what is happening with us.

6. 1v46-56 Mary praises God

Informing:
  • About 2000 years before this, God had promised Abraham that through his descendants there would be a source of blessing for all the nations. The nation that came from his grandson, Jacob (whose name was changed to Israel) had a special place in the plans and promises of God being fulfilled. There are many things that God promised about "Israel" that happened through Jesus.

Introducing:
  • It is clear that Mary was very happy! Nothing will make us happier than being joined with Jesus in God's plans.
  • Just as God noticed Mary, so he notices us.
  • Jesus wants us to know him as Mary knew him – not as a saviour, or as the Saviour, but as my Saviour.

Inspiring:
  • The Holy Spirit, through the words that Mary said, gives us a picture of what God is like:
  God is active. He is doing things in the world.
  He has big plans that he is working out.
  He cares and so he does things that show how he feels.
  He is interested in making ordinary people happy.
  He keeps his promises.

Instructing:
  • God is working out his plans, and they are big plans. His plans for us are linked with what he has done in the past and also with what he wants to do in the future.
  • We can trust God's Word. He will do what he has said.
  • Sometimes we can see what God is doing, while at other times we do not know what he is doing. Sometimes we can feel as if God has forgotten us and that he has not done what he has promised. But he still has us in mind and he is going to keep all his promises, even if it takes 2000 years of

plans and work to do it.

• God is still looking for those like Mary who are willing to be his humble servants.

7. 1v57-66 John is born and named

Informing:
• To circumcise means "to cut round". Jewish baby boys had a little piece of the spare skin cut from the end of their penis as a sign that they were part of God's specially chosen people. Being God's chosen people does not mean that the people of Israel were God's favourites, but rather that God had a special agreement with them from the time of Abraham to show his Kingdom to the rest of the world through them. This meant that they had special responsibilities in the way they lived.
• The name, "John" means "God's gift". John was a special gift to his parents, and his life would be about telling people about God's extra-special gift, Jesus.

Introducing:
• The people wondered what this child would become. Special things were happening in his life because he was linked to Jesus. They saw something of God's plans, but they would have to wait about 30 years to see the very special place that John had.

Inspiring:
• There are many different ways that people react when the Holy Spirit is at work.
It is mentioned here that: they rejoiced, they were surprised, astonished, they were afraid, they talked about it, they wondered what might happen, and they recognised that God was at work.

Instructing:
• The people made signs to communicate with Zechariah, so it looks as if for more than nine months he was unable to hear, along with being unable to speak. Beware of not believing what God says to you! This can lead us to not hearing from God and not being able to speak for God.
• The relatives and neighbours had their ideas about the boy and what he should be called, but his father knew what God had said about him. Other people may have ideas of who <u>you</u> are and what they expect you to

27

do, but the most important thing for us is to hear the ideas that God has for us and to live for that.

• If our lives are linked with Jesus then the Lord's hand will be with us to make a difference in our lives, and people will see that, even if they may not always understand it.

8. 1v67-80 Zechariah praises God

Informing:
  • "Prophesying" means speaking out the words that God is giving to say. These words can show what God is like, what God feels, what God has done, is doing, is going to do, and what God wants people to do.
  • The prophets whose words we read in the Old Testament were given special messages, not just for the people of their time, but also to help people at a later time to understand and be ready for what God was going to do.
  • John was called a prophet as he was going to do that work too.

Introducing:
  • Here it is announced that God has promised to save, and that Jesus is coming to do it: to set people free from being controlled and overpowered, to protect them from harmful attack, to rescue them from danger, and to bring them out from fear, darkness and death into the peace of a new day.

Inspiring:
  • Because these words that Zechariah spoke came by him being filled with the Holy Spirit, they promised even more than what people hoped would happen. God's plans are greater and better than we can imagine.
  • Even though at this point Jesus had not yet been born, the words read as if Jesus had already done everything. That is because when the Holy Spirit says something, it is as good as done. When God says what he has decided to do, nothing is going to stop it happening.

Instructing:
  • God wants us to be able to serve him without being afraid, and to be saved from anything that would stop us doing that. We might think that God would do that by removing our enemies or changing them, instead he does it by removing our sin and changing us. Living in God's forgiveness is how we can serve him without fear.
  • There were many years of John's life when it was not obvious that God was using him for anything special. Times like that can be for us, like

they were for him, opportunities to be made strong for what God is going to do through us in the future.

9. 2v1-20 Jesus is born

Informing:
- Augustus was the leader of the Roman Empire which at that time had taken over and ruled Israel and much of the world, including Britain.
- The census was the taking of a register of people's names in the countries which the Romans governed so that they would pay taxes.
- David in the Old Testament (1 Samuel 16) was looking after sheep near Bethlehem when he was called to Bethlehem to be recognised as God's chosen King. The shepherds looking after sheep near Bethlehem are here being called to Bethlehem to recognise Jesus as God's chosen King.

Introducing:
- Who appeared to the shepherds? An angel of <u>the Lord.</u>
- What shone round them? The glory of <u>the Lord.</u>
- Who did they say had given them the message? "<u>The Lord</u> told us."
- Who is <u>the Lord</u>? God.
- Who were they told had been born? Christ, <u>the Lord.</u>
- If <u>the Lord</u> is God, and Jesus is <u>the Lord</u>, then Jesus is God.

Inspiring:
- The Holy Spirit works in many different ways to get things done.
- The Holy Spirit is working <u>through events</u>. The government's census meant that Joseph and Mary were in Bethlehem, where, according to prophecy given hundreds of years before, God's specially chosen one (the Messiah, the Christ) would be born.
- The Holy Spirit is working <u>through angels</u> - special messengers from heaven.
- The Holy Spirit is working <u>through shepherds</u> - ordinary people who pass on God's message to Mary, Joseph and others.

Instructing:
- We never know when, like the boy David or the shepherds here, we may be doing something which is completely ordinary, and God will focus

his attention on us to bring us into having a part in his special plans.

• God is looking for those who are available to him.

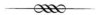

10. 2v21-40 Simeon and Anna meet Jesus

Informing:

• After a baby was born, a Jewish mother was to bring the child and offer two sacrifices to God – a lamb and a pigeon. If she was not able to bring a lamb she could bring another pigeon. In doing this she was bringing herself and her baby to God in an act of worship. (This is described in Leviticus chapter 12.)

• A first son was to be brought in a special act of worship as a reminder and a sign that the Israelites belonged to God from the time when God took the Israelites out of slavery in Egypt with Moses. Because Pharaoh, the king of Egypt, had refused to allow them to leave, in one night God killed all the oldest sons of the Egyptians but he spared all the first-born children of the Israelites. (The account of this is in Exodus chapters 11 and 12.)

• Luke does not know everything about Jesus' life, so he does not mention the visit of the wise men or the time that Joseph, Mary and Jesus spent in Egypt before they returned to Nazareth (Matthew chapter 2).

Introducing:

• Jesus had come as "the Christ" which means "the anointed one". ("The Messiah" means the same.) In the Old Testament, when someone was anointed (had oil poured on them), it showed that they were God's specially chosen person to be a king or a prophet or a priest.

• The "Christ" or "Messiah" was the promised extra-special person the Jews were waiting for. Most people in other nations did not know about the promised Messiah, but Simeon makes it clear that although Jesus came <u>to</u> the Israelites, he did not come just <u>for</u> them but to be God's saving plan for <u>all</u> the nations. "Gentiles" is the word sometimes used for the non-Jewish nations.

Inspiring:

• Simeon's experience of the Holy Spirit is a good example of what we can expect in our lives:

The Holy Spirit was upon him - with him in his daily life.

The Holy Spirit showed him things that he could not have known otherwise.

The Holy Spirit helped him to know Jesus better.

The Holy Spirit gave him words from God to say to help others.

Instructing:

• The clear lesson here is: Be faithful!

• Mary and Joseph were faithful in doing everything that God's law required.

• Simeon was faithful in receiving what God had said to him and in following the leading of the Holy Spirit.

• Anna was faithful throughout her life in serving God.

The result was that they had an experience of Jesus that was worth waiting for, and were able to bless each other and others too.

• Jesus grew up faithful to all he was meant to be.

11. 2v41-52 Jesus talks in the temple

Informing:
• The Passover Festival was a celebration of how God took the Israelites out of slavery in Egypt in the time of Moses. In it there was a special family meal in which the family learned and were reminded of what God had done. They had the same type of meal and did what the Israelites had done on the night when they left Egypt. (There is more about the Passover in *Informing:* 82. 21v37-22v23.)

Introducing:
• When we wonder how parents could travel a whole day before realising that their son was not with them, it helps to know that Jesus was part of a big family. In Matthew 13v55,56 we are told that Jesus had four brothers and at least three sisters.
• Jesus was now at the age when he was expected to take responsibility for his own actions. In the years before this, he had gone to the temple with his parents because his parents had decided they were going. This time he chose to stay at the temple because now he was able to decide for himself.
• This is the first time in the story of Jesus' life that we have words that Jesus said. They show us that he knew clearly who he was, as he spoke of God as "my Father".

Inspiring:
• Just as the Holy Spirit had led Zechariah, and then Simeon and Anna to be in the temple at a particular time, now the Holy Spirit leads Jesus there to share with the teachers his special understanding from his relationship with God.
• Then, after this special experience, the Holy Spirit leads him back to the ordinary life of going back home and fitting in with his parents.
• The Holy Spirit's plans for us will involve some extraordinary experiences, and a lot of ordinary experiences.

Instructing:

• When we want to live for God, to do what he wants and to follow the leading of the Holy Spirit, it will at times mean that, like Jesus, we are doing something different from the group we are part of. Sometimes even those who are close to us may not understand fully why we are doing what we have chosen to do.

• We should remember too that Jesus will at times do things that are different from what we would expect. When we decide on what we are going to do, we should check to make sure that we are with Jesus every day, and that we have not left him behind and gone ahead without thinking about him.

12. 3v1-20 John the Baptist preaches

Informing:
- Sons of Abraham - see *Informing:* 7. 1v57-66
- Tax collecting - see *Informing:* 22. 5v27-32
- The words in verses 4-6 are from Isaiah chapter 40 in the Old Testament.
- Whatever is happening with countries, rulers and governments, the most important difference is made by people who are in touch with God, people like John to whom God's message came.
- Since Bible times, churches have introduced different practices in baptising people. The word "to baptise" properly means to dip, like when putting dishes into water to wash them. So it means being in water, being put under the water and being brought back out of the water.
- In 1961 a stone with words on it was found in Israel. It had Pilate's name on it, and it shows that he had the position and authority as governor of Judea that Luke says he had.

Introducing:
- People thought that John was special, and he was, as he was the person who had been prophesied by Isaiah 700 years before. He was the one to help get things ready for the even more special person who was coming. In Isaiah chapter 40 where the words in verses 4-6 come from, it makes it clear that the one who is coming is the Lord. That means God.
- Jesus coming to baptise with the Holy Spirit means that he would bring the power for people to live in God's way.
- Jesus coming to baptise with fire means that he would bring the power to destroy things that are against us living in God's way.

Inspiring:
- The Holy Spirit gave the message to Isaiah, then after 700 years of history and 30 years of John's life the exact right time came to fulfil God's plan. The Holy Spirit has exact times to guide things in our lives to fit in with God's plans.
- It must have been clear that the Holy Spirit was with John, because

people believed what he said and obeyed his message.

• When God gives words to be said, he gives his Spirit too, so that what he says can then happen.

Instructing:

• When God is doing special things in people's lives, others can sometimes want to join in what is happening without understanding fully what it means. So people can sometimes want to be baptised because others are being baptised, or because someone expects them to, or because they don't want to be left out.

• Being baptised means that you not only want God's forgiveness, but that you are ready for your life to be changed by Jesus, and that you are ready to do what God wants. This is what is meant by the word "repentance" which is used in verse 3. It means a change of mind that leads to a change in what you do.

13. 3v21-38 John baptises Jesus

Informing:
- We are given no details of what happened in Jesus' life from when he was 12 at the temple to when he was baptised at about 30 years old. What we know is: He lived in Nazareth. His "father" Joseph was a carpenter (Matthew 13v55) and so was he (Mark 6v3). He was the oldest of a big family with four brothers and at least three sisters (Matthew 13v55,56). By the time Jesus began his preaching, teaching and healing work, Joseph had died as he is not mentioned when Jesus' family is talked about (Mark 3v21,31).
- The Messiah was to come from King David's descendants. Matthew, in his book (Matthew 1v1-17), gives Joseph's family line, and Luke gives Joseph's "in-laws", that is Mary's family line. Both lines meet in David.

Introducing:
- In the temple when he was 12 years old, Jesus was, in a way, saying, "You are my Father", and here at about 30 years old, when he is being baptised, Father is saying, "You are my son". Father has been pleased with how Jesus has lived when he has been growing up and working in the ordinary job of being a carpenter. Now, Jesus, by being baptised is saying that he is ready for whatever his Father wants next.

Inspiring:
- The things that happened at Jesus' baptism show Father, Son and Holy Spirit working together.
- It is only upon Jesus that the Holy Spirit is said to come in a way that looked like a dove.
- John the Baptist had been told by God (John 1v32-34) that he would see the Holy Spirit come down and stay on someone. That was to be the sign that this person was the Son of God.
- We are not told why the Holy Spirit came in the shape of a dove. We may get a clue from the other places in the Bible where a dove is mentioned. After the world was "baptised" in the flood, when the dove went out of the ark and found a place to stay, this showed that a new time

had begun (Genesis 8v8-12). So after Jesus was baptised, when the Holy Spirit "dove" went from heaven and found a place to stay on Jesus, this showed that another new time had begun.

Instructing:
  • We can please our heavenly Father by our ordinary family lives, also by taking special steps such as being baptised, and by saying yes to his plans for our lives.

14. 4v1-15 Jesus is tempted

Informing:
   • The name "Satan" means someone who is against us. It is another name for the Devil in the Bible.
   • The Devil is a real enemy. He tries to spoil our relationship with our heavenly Father. He tries to get us to do things his way rather than God's way. He tries to get us to misuse what God has said.
   • The last verse of the previous chapter (3v38) mentions Adam. Adam failed when the Devil tempted him and sin came into the world. The account of this is in Genesis chapter 3. Now, here we have Jesus, the one who has come to take sin away, facing the same Devil and winning.

Introducing:
   • Jesus here faced all the attempts of the Devil to turn him away from what he had come to do. For 40 days the Devil put suggestions to him to try to break his commitment to his Father. We now know that the Devil can be beaten and that we don't have to give in to his temptations because Jesus was tempted in every way as we are but did not sin.
   • It was a tough time for Jesus. He had just heard his Father say that he loved him and was pleased with him, and then he was immediately put out into the desert with no food for 40 days to face continual trouble from the Devil. But Jesus stayed faithful to his Father and he won the battle against the Devil!

Inspiring:
   • The Holy Spirit came upon Jesus, the Holy Spirit filled Jesus, the Holy Spirit led Jesus, and the Holy Spirit worked in power through Jesus.
   • When the Holy Spirit comes upon us he wants to fill us.
   • When the Holy Spirit fills us he wants to lead us.
   • When the Holy Spirit leads us he wants to work in power through us.

Instructing:
   • We are not meant to give in to the Devil's suggestions. We have Jesus' example to follow to keep us from going the wrong way.

• Being committed to God, we can know that he is committed to us.

• Getting to know what God has said in the Bible will lead us to know how he wants us to live, so that we will be able to see when ideas come to us that are against what he has said.

• If we are being filled with the Holy Spirit and letting the Holy Spirit lead us, we will find that when we go through tough times he will always be there to take us through them in the right way.

15. 4v16-30 Jesus preaches at Nazareth

Informing:
  • The synagogue was like a local church where Jews met to worship, pray and be taught.
    • The word "synagogue" means a gathering – a bringing together.
    • The passage Jesus read is from Isaiah 61.
    • The passage with Elijah and the widow is in 1 Kings 17.
    • The passage with Elisha and Naaman is in 2 Kings 5.

Introducing:
  • Jesus says that what had been written by a prophet 700 years before was written about him. Jesus is the focus of all God's plans, so all that we read in the Bible has some connection with him. If we understand passages of the Bible correctly, they will help us to know Jesus better and teach us how to live for him.
  • Jesus speaks about himself as being a doctor and a prophet. As a doctor he wants to make people whole, but he can only heal those who will come to him to be made well. As a prophet he says some wonderful words of God's love which people like, but he does not hold back from saying what God wants to be said, even when people will not like it.

Inspiring:
  • The Holy Spirit was with Jesus in a very special way, because Jesus was the "Anointed"- (the Christ).
  • As Christians, we too have the Holy Spirit with us to do the things he did with Jesus. He will give us words to say, show us where to say them, when to say them, how to say them, and he will give us protection!
  • For the Holy Spirit to use us as he used Jesus, we will need to know the Bible well.

Instructing:
  • We should beware of the Nazareth mistake! That is the mistake of thinking that it is only our group and our way of doing things that God likes and will bless. That idea has been held by many "Christians" but it is

43

totally against Jesus' Kingdom and has been the cause of terrible things being done.

• The people of Nazareth did not like Jesus suggesting that some people they did not approve of might be more open to God than they were. They did not like it, but it was true.

• We should remember that there are many people outside the church who may be more ready to receive what Jesus wants to say and do than some who go to church.

16. 4v31-37 Jesus stops an evil spirit

Informing:
• Jesus went to live in Capernaum (a town beside the Sea of Galilee) and used it as a base from which he travelled around the area.
• This passage has the first mention by Luke about evil spirits, sometimes called unclean spirits or demons. There is much more about them in later parts of the book.

Introducing:
• When Jesus commanded the evil spirit to leave the man, it was clear that Jesus had <u>power</u> because something happened when he spoke – the evil spirit went!
• But even before that happened, the people recognised that Jesus spoke with <u>authority</u> when he taught. To have authority is to have the right to do what you are doing. The people saw that Jesus was sure of what he was telling them, and he said things in a way that challenged them to obey what he was saying.

Inspiring:
• The Holy Spirit looks for places and people's lives where he can do what God wants to be done.
• Evil spirits look for places and people's lives where they can do what the Devil wants and where they can oppose all that God wants to happen.
• When the Holy Spirit comes in power (as he did in Jesus) to a place or a person's life, this can cause a reaction from any evil spirit which has had some influence in that place or person. Things which have been hidden are brought into the open, as happened with this man in the synagogue.

Instructing:
• Jesus spoke with authority and power because he always did what Father wanted, and because he was living in line with the Holy Spirit.
• If we want to help to free people from the power of evil in their lives, we should be growing in following Jesus' example in the way that we live.

Then when we say the things that the Holy Spirit gives us to say, it will make a difference to the place we are in and the people we are with.

17. 4v38-41 Jesus heals at Simon's house

Informing:
- This passage has the first mention by Luke about Simon.
- Simon had first met Jesus after Jesus' baptism (John1v35-42) when he had been introduced to him by Andrew, Simon's brother. Jesus had given Simon the name "Peter" which means a rock
- Then one day (Mark 1v16-29), Jesus had called Simon away from fishing, along with Andrew and James and John. They were together with Jesus in the synagogue and in Simon's house.

Introducing:
- In freeing the man from an evil spirit in the synagogue, and freeing Simon's mother-in-law from a fever at home, it is as if Jesus is opening a door for healing in Capernaum. The people there are happy to come through the "open door" to receive what Jesus was able to give. What happiness there must have been in the town that night! What a contrast with Nazareth where Jesus had "opened a door" for all that he had come to do and the people had slammed it shut.
- No doubt many in Nazareth felt as Jesus said they would, "Why didn't he do here the things we have heard about him doing in Capernaum?" The answer was simple – they did not receive him, while those in Capernaum did.

Inspiring:
- What evil, unclean, unholy spirits want is to oppose the work of the Holy Spirit.
- Even when they say things that are true, as when they recognised Jesus as the Son of God, they want to use it to serve the Devil and to get people to disobey God.
- Remember what the Devil did when he tempted Jesus. He said that if Jesus was the Son of God (right and true) he should command the stone to turn into bread (wrong).
- When evil spirits came into contact with Jesus, even though they hated it, they had to accept his authority and the authority of the Holy

47

Spirit in him.

• Jesus silenced them from saying any more because they would want to use the information for the Devil's purposes. They would want to say more and confuse the people who were listening and could hear them.

• Jesus was not looking to be famous. He was looking to do what his Father wanted. Sometimes being "famous" could make that more difficult. You will see this in *Instructing:* 20. 5v12-16.

Instructing:

• Peter and his family spoke to Jesus about his mother-in-law. The people healed by Jesus were brought to him by friends. When we have family members or friends who are in need of healing, we can talk to Jesus about them and put them in touch with him.

18. 4v42-44 Jesus goes to different towns

Informing:
• This is the first of many times that Luke mentions Jesus speaking about the Kingdom of God. Jesus says that he is bringing the Good News of God's Kingdom, to show what things can be like when God rules. We know what this is like from what Jesus said in the Nazareth synagogue about what he was sent to do (4v18,19).

Introducing:
• Although we can talk to God at any time and in any place, we see here that it was important to Jesus to find times and places where he could be away from everyone else to take time to pray. The place that he found was good for this was out in the countryside.

Inspiring:
• Jesus described himself as being on a Holy Spirit mission. In Nazareth he had said that the Spirit of the Lord was upon him and had sent him. Here he says that there was something he must do because that is what he had been sent to do.
• Jesus was going to stick to the Holy Spirit plan, even when it meant leaving a lot of people who wanted him to stay, and doing something which was different from what they and those with him expected.
• Although it may have looked a strange decision to leave those people, the Holy Spirit and Jesus were not abandoning them. Jesus came back later to that town and taught them. The events of 5v17-26 happened in the same place. Mark, in his book, (Mark 1v21; Mark 2v1), mentions that both these things happened in Capernaum.

Instructing:
• Jesus' example here is one of the most important lessons for our lives – to do only what the Holy Spirit is giving us to do, even when it seems that we could be serving God by doing something else that others want us to do.
• Also, when we know what the Holy Spirit is giving us to do, in order to

be prepared for it, we should take time to be on our own with God.

• When we see the power of Jesus being demonstrated in a place, we should not think that things are going to continue there in the same way. Along with rejoicing in what Jesus has done and is doing, we should be looking for, and be ready for what Jesus wants to do next. He may surprise us!

19. 5v1-11 Jesus calls some fishermen

Informing:

• Lake Gennesaret is another name for the Sea of Galilee.

• Simon, James and John were already followers of Jesus. At a time before this, (Mark 1v14-20), Simon and his brother, Andrew were fishing, and James and John were getting their nets ready. Jesus had called them and they had left what they were doing to learn from him. This day, they were not just leaving what they were doing at the time; they were leaving being fishermen to be part of a team working with Jesus.

• There is an interesting "follow-up" story to this one in John 21.

• In verse 1 and in other places in Luke's book the Word of God is mentioned. This does not mean just words or descriptions about God; it means the communicating, expressing and explaining of what God thinks.

Introducing:

• Jesus speaks words from God in teaching the crowd and shows the power of God in the miraculous catch of fish.

• When Jesus gives the fishermen a miracle in the part of life they know best (catching fish), what is he showing them?

1) If you lend your boat to me, you won't miss out.

2) My power goes far beyond natural ability.

3) You have relied on fishing to meet your needs; you can now rely on me to meet your needs.

4) You will catch people for God's Kingdom in the same way as you caught these fish, by doing what I tell you to do, where I tell you to do it, and when I tell you to do it.

5) Just as I took the step of doing what the Holy Spirit said, even when it meant leaving behind a big "catch" of people (4v42-44), so now it is time for you to take that sort of step, and leave behind a big catch of fish to do what God wants.

• It says that they left everything and went with him, which means that they left behind two boatloads of fish! Presumably that was looked after by people like Zebedee and the hired men who were mentioned in Mark 1 as working with them.

Inspiring:

• There is a Holy Spirit move in the crowd; they push to get close to Jesus because they want to hear the Word of God.

• There is a Holy Spirit move in Simon Peter; he realises that Jesus' great power is linked to his great purity, and Peter sees his own impurity.

• There is a Holy Spirit move in the fishermen which makes them free to leave everything and go with Jesus.

Instructing:

• Peter's example shows us how we can move on with Jesus. When told to push out a <u>little</u>, he said a simple "yes" to what he had (a boat) being used by Jesus.

• When told to push out <u>further</u>, he did not understand why Jesus wanted him to let down the nets, but he did it.

• When given the opportunity to go <u>even</u> <u>further</u> with Jesus, Peter accepted Jesus' words to him to not be afraid, and left other things behind to go on with him.

20. 5v12-16 Jesus heals a man with leprosy

Informing:
- Leprosy is a disease caught by touching someone who has it. Skin becomes discoloured, hard and lumpy. Fingers and toes go stiff and bent and lose the feeling of pain, so they then get injured.
- God had told Moses that people with skin diseases had to stay away from others. This was to prevent others from catching what might be deadly diseases for which there was no cure at that time. It would be difficult to tell whether a skin disease was one that would pass or would be long-lasting and serious. If the disease seemed to have passed, the person had to go to a priest who would examine him. If the disease had passed, the priest would say the person was clean from it and he would lead the person in a special service to mark his recovery. (Leviticus 14v1-31)

Introducing:
- The man believed that Jesus was a very special person. He called him, "Lord" and he bowed down to the ground before him. Even though he was full of the disease, he believed that Jesus had the power to heal him. He also believed that Jesus would want to heal him. He was right! We never read of anyone who came to Jesus that he did not have the power to heal or that he did not want to heal.

Inspiring:
- Healing is a gift of the Holy Spirit; it is a gift of God's love.
- When Jesus touched the man (something that everyone else would have avoided), instead of the disease going from the man to Jesus, healing power went from Jesus into the man. It was a very powerful gift. The man changed from having his skin covered in disease, to having completely healthy skin!
- The Holy Spirit in us gives us power stronger than anything we come up against.

Instructing:

• The man believed in Jesus, he was healed by Jesus but he did not obey Jesus. Mark's account in Mark 1v40-45 shows that he disobeyed Jesus by not going to the priest but went telling many people. We would usually think that it was a good idea to tell many people what Jesus has done for us, but as happened in this case, we can sometimes miss what is best by doing what we think rather than what Jesus wants.

By not obeying:

1) He missed the opportunity of bringing his sacrifice of thanksgiving and worship in the special service that would have been held.

2) He missed the opportunity to tell the priest and show him what Jesus had done, so he missed the very person that Jesus wanted to hear about it.

3) He made things difficult for Jesus. Jesus' plan was to teach, preach and heal in the towns, and have a place to pray in the countryside. Now people came out to him in the countryside.

4) He made things difficult for those who were most ill in the towns because they would not be able to get to Jesus in the countryside.

• May we not repeat his mistake; our enthusiasm should not take the place of our obedience.

21. 5v17-26 A paralysed man is carried to Jesus

Informing:
- "Teachers of the Law", otherwise known as "Scribes" (which means writers), were religious Jews who studied the books of Moses (Genesis, Exodus, Leviticus, Numbers and Deuteronomy). Starting from the laws that God gave, they made up instructions to cover every part of life. They taught that these instructions were how to live according to God's law.
- The Pharisees were people who committed themselves to living according to these strict instructions. Their name means "separate", and they kept away from people who did not live like they did, because they thought of such people as unclean.
- Although it looks like a good commitment to try to obey God in every detail of life, the Scribes and the Pharisees were very proud and far away from what God wanted.

Introducing:
- Enough had happened through Jesus to make people come from all over the country to see him and hear him, and their big question was, "Who is this?" (v21)
- Jesus described himself as "the Son of Man". This shows that he is both ordinary and special. He is ordinary: son of man, human, not a heavenly angel. He is special: he is the Son of Man. He is the one who is living as God wants people to live, and is doing and saying what God wants. He is God's special agent.
- "The Son of Man" is the name that Jesus used most often about himself. This is the first of 26 times in Luke's book.

Inspiring:
- The Holy Spirit's power is given to help us do what God wants done.
- God wants people to be healed, so the power of the Holy Spirit is there to do it.
- God wants people to receive forgiveness for their sins, and the power of the Holy Spirit comes through the words of Jesus.

• God wants people's wrong ideas to be put right, so by the Holy Spirit's power, Jesus knows what they are thinking.

Instructing:
• The man and his friends give us a good lesson in faith:

1) They <u>believed</u> that Jesus could and would heal him.

2) They <u>decided</u> together to bring him to Jesus.

3) They <u>came</u>, carrying the man who was not able to come on his own.

4) They <u>tried</u> to get to Jesus.

5) They could not find a way through. (Would we have given up at this point?)

6) They <u>refused to give up</u>, and they got through to Jesus because they were determined to find a way.

• The result was that everyone saw God in action in a special way, and here we are reading about it 2000 years later!

22. 5v27-32 A tax collector becomes a disciple

Informing:

• Tax collectors were not liked because they worked for the Romans who had taken over and were governing Israel. Tax collectors were considered to be unfaithful to their own people because they worked for "the enemy". They were considered to be unclean because they mixed with people who were not Jews, and they made money by overcharging people when they taxed them. The Roman government would charge a set amount for goods being grown, bought and sold, or transported, and it was the job of the tax collectors to collect this money.

• This tax collector, Levi, is also known as Matthew.

• Verse 30 is the first time that Luke uses the word "disciple" to describe those who were with Jesus. The word means "learner" but it means more than a pupil or student. A pupil may learn and then answer questions in an exam, but a disciple is learning from someone's teaching and then putting it into practice, so that what the disciple is doing is in line with the thinking of the person who is teaching him.

Introducing:

• Jesus wants to make people whole. When he spends time with people or calls a particular person, this does not mean that he approves of what they are or what they do. He does it because he is committed to what they can become by being with him. Jesus is happy to be alongside any person who will allow him to change them into all that God wants them to be.

Inspiring:

• Levi responded straight away when Jesus called him simply to follow him. This suggests that he already wanted to be a follower of Jesus. Levi was working in Capernaum where Jesus was based so he would have had some opportunities to know what Jesus was doing. If he wanted to be a follower of Jesus, but had not yet become one, why was that? It was probably because he thought that someone like him would not be accepted. So the Holy Spirit arranged for him to hear the simple words that he needed to hear to let him know that Jesus really wanted <u>him</u> to be with him.

• The Holy Spirit will arrange for us to hear the words that we need to hear.

Instructing:

• When a church minister in the west of Scotland was asked why he did the work he did, he said, "I want my community to be loved like I am". It looks as if Levi felt like that. When he left his well paid job to follow Jesus, Levi did not think that doing this was a great sacrifice, but rather a reason to celebrate. He had a big party to share his celebration with others.

• When we obey Jesus' call on our lives, it will mean leaving other things behind, but it will also mean having the privilege of being alongside Jesus in what he is doing, and being used to help others to know that they too are wanted by Jesus.

23. 5v33-39 Jesus answers a question

Informing:
- Parables - see *Informing:* 35. 8v4-21
- Fasting is having a time of not eating.
- Jesus had times of fasting. When dealing with the Devil in the desert, Jesus ate nothing for 40 days (4v1). When healing the boy who had an evil spirit, Jesus said that it could only be dealt with by prayer and fasting (Matthew 17v21).
- Jesus expected his followers to have personal times of fasting. In Matthew 6v16, Jesus says that when they fasted it was not something to make a show of, but to do quietly as part of serving God, like when praying and giving.
- Times of fasting were held by groups of God's people in the Old Testament and New Testament as part of coming to God and looking for God to do something in a time of particular need. Fasting was not given as something that had to be done as a religious duty like, for instance, the sacrifices were.

Introducing:
- Jesus describes himself as a bridegroom. This is how John the Baptist had spoken about him. In John 3v29 John the Baptist said that the Messiah is the bridegroom, and that he, John, was the bridegroom's friend, happy at his coming. This is also how Jesus is described at the end of the Bible (Revelation 19v5-9), where heaven is seen as his special wedding party.
- Jesus also shows in what he says that he already knows about his death, as he mentions the time when he will be taken away from his people.

Inspiring:
- The Holy Spirit has different things for different people to do at different times. There were some special things that the Holy Spirit had for John the Baptist to do. Then the Holy Spirit had some different special things for Jesus to do.
- It was right for the group with Jesus to be celebrating at this time. It

would be right for the group to be doing something different at another time.

• The important thing for us is to know what the Holy Spirit is leading us to do, and to do what he is leading us to do.

Instructing:

• Like Jesus, we should be able to say why we are doing the things we are doing, and why we are not doing the things that we are not doing!

• The picture of a new patch on old clothing and new wine in old containers is describing how useful things can be spoiled by being mixed together when they are meant to be kept separate. We should recognise and respect the different ways that others have of serving God, without trying to change them to fit in with us, and without moving away from what we are being led to do.

• We should be careful not to be so fixed in what we are doing that we miss the new ways in which the Holy Spirit may be beginning to work. We are right to appreciate what God has done in the past (the old wine). We are not right if as a result we do not appreciate the different things God wants to do now (the new wine).

24. 6v1-11 Pharisees criticise Jesus

Informing:

• The Sabbath, a weekly day of rest, was given by God to be a blessing. The Teachers of the Law and the Pharisees had made it into a burden by making up rules which they said people had to obey if they were to keep the Sabbath. They argued like this:

On the Sabbath, working is wrong, so harvesting a field is wrong. Picking ears of corn is harvesting, so it is work, so it is wrong.

• In the story about David, King Saul was jealous of David being God's chosen person and wanted to kill him. (This looks like the way in which the Pharisees were being jealous of Jesus.) David ran away to avoid Saul. David and his men asked the priest for some food. The only food that was available was special bread that usually only priests ate. The Pharisees would accept that the person in authority, David, had the right to set aside the normal following of God's instructions in special circumstances.

They believed that they had the authority to do that too. Jesus is telling them that <u>he</u> has the authority to decide the right way to do what God wants, and that they should recognise that.

Introducing:

• Jesus makes his second "The Son of Man" statement. He has already said that the Son of Man has authority to forgive sins, and now he says he is the Lord of the Sabbath. These are things that people would only have said about God.

• The Pharisees tried to catch Jesus out by him working on the Sabbath by healing someone. They considered healing someone to be "work". What work would they have expected? Probably they would have thought that he would examine, take hold of the affected part, talk and pray about the condition, and they would consider that to be "work". But Jesus catches them out. He calls the man to stand in the middle and stretch out his hand, and without Jesus doing any "work" the man is healed! No wonder the Pharisees were angry at him!

Inspiring:

• The Holy Spirit can help us learn lessons from the Bible – like Jesus teaching from the story about David.

• He can help us to know what is right for us to do – we do not just have to obey rules that others have made up.

• The Holy Spirit can help us to know what is in people's hearts – like Jesus knowing what they were thinking.

• He can help us to help others with his power – like when the man was healed.

• The Holy Spirit can help us to keep doing things in Jesus' way when people are against us.

Instructing:

• We should practise loving people rather than criticising them, and think what we can do to help them. Instead of criticising Jesus' followers for picking corn, the Pharisees, if they had really been trying to serve God, should have given them a meal because they were hungry! Instead of waiting to see whether Jesus would heal on the Sabbath, they should have taken the man to Jesus to be healed – before the Sabbath if they wanted!

• However, being loving does not mean that we should change what we do in order to be accepted by those who are against Jesus.

25. 6v12-19 Jesus chooses twelve apostles

Informing:

• Pharisees and Teachers of the Law had come from all over the country to investigate Jesus (5v17) but now crowds of people come from all over the country and beyond to receive from Jesus. Those who came from Sidon had come about 50 miles, and those who had come from Jerusalem had come about 80 miles. That is a long way to come as they did, either on a donkey, or walking or being carried to be healed!

• There are 3 groups of people in the passage:

1) The crowds who go to Jesus to get (to hear and be healed).

2) Disciples (learners) who go with Jesus to grow (to know him better and become like him).

3) Apostles (which means "sent ones") who go for Jesus to give (to give to others what Jesus gives).

Introducing:

• Jesus' plan (choosing a team for special work) and his power (healing the crowds) come after his prayer.

• It is a well-timed night of prayer as Jesus is about to:

1) appoint a team of apostles – those he will send to work for him.

2) give teaching to a crowd of disciples – those who wanted to learn by being with him.

3) heal great crowds of people – those who were in need of his power to change them.

Inspiring:

• The Holy Spirit has particular jobs for particular people to do. We don't need to have any special qualifications. The team of apostles was made up of a mixture of ordinary people.

• The Holy Spirit gives different jobs to individuals so that they can work well together.

• When the people are being healed, a word used means that power was coming out "from alongside" Jesus and healing them. Jesus described the Holy Spirit as the one "called alongside", and he is given to us (John 14v16,17).

Instructing:

• If we want to be an apostle (one sent to work for Jesus), we must first be a disciple, learning from spending time with Jesus. The apostles were chosen from those who were already disciples.

• If we are not chosen for a particular work that others are chosen for, God still has special plans for us. In Acts 1, we read of Matthias who had been one of the crowd of disciples who went everywhere with Jesus. Later, after Jesus went back to heaven, Matthias was made one of the apostles!

• There are "waiting times" in God's plans, like in being a disciple before being an apostle. Also, here Jesus appoints the apostles but there is a time gap before they are sent out (9v1,2). Waiting times can be useful for us to be prepared for what God wants us to do.

26. 6v20-40 Jesus teaches about happiness

Informing:

• Jesus said these words to the crowd of disciples, not just to the twelve. These words are not only about special leaders. They are for all those who are learning from Jesus and who want to be like him, so these words are about you.

• Many times in the Old Testament people had rejected the prophets. That was because, as part of telling people how they could live in God's blessing, they had to tell people where they had chosen to go wrong and had left God's way.

Introducing:

• Jesus is showing us what he wants us to be. He wants us, as children of God (v35) to be like our heavenly Father, and to be like Jesus, our teacher (v40). He knows that we cannot be like him immediately but he expects us to grow to be like him.

• Words that Jesus uses to show what it means to be like him are: be happy, love, do good, pray, give, be merciful, and forgive. These things do not depend on what is happening around us or on what other people are doing. These things come as our response to what God is doing in our lives.

Inspiring:

• How can we live like Jesus talks about here? There is only one way, and that is if we have the Holy Spirit working in our lives. If we are committed to learning to live like Jesus wants us to, God will give us all that we need to do it. We will be able to give to others because we have received from the Holy Spirit.

Instructing:

• Two reasons are given by Jesus for following the instructions he gives us here. Firstly, we will become like him, and secondly we will receive a great reward from God.

• The Devil tries to get people to believe that they will have more by going their own way than they would if they went God's way. That is the

Devil's lie – it is never true.

• However bad things may seem, and however badly we are being treated, if we are living for Jesus, whatever it is costing us will be more than made up for by him. There is much more coming to us than we have received so far. As Jesus' disciples we are living for what is to come.

27. 6v41-49 Jesus instructs his followers

Informing:
- When Jesus warns us here not to be hypocrites, he uses a word that describes actors in a play – doing the actions, putting on a show, wearing a mask, pretending to be something that they are not in real life.

Introducing:
- Jesus wants to guard people from missing out on being all that they can be when they know him and live for him.
- He uses many ways to communicate his message:

Questions - "Why do you…?"

Challenging words - "hypocrite".

Fun - the idea of someone with a log in their eye trying to help someone with a speck of dust in theirs.

Pictures - about trees and fruit.

Stories - about the men building the houses.

- He points out where we might go wrong, not to show us that we fail, but to help us to succeed.

Inspiring:
- The Holy Spirit will help us to be everything that Jesus wants us to be.
- If we want to obey Jesus, the Holy Spirit will make us able to help others, so that they can see the truth clearly.
- The Holy Spirit will make us fruitful, with lives overflowing with God's goodness in what we do and say.
- The Holy Spirit will make us unshakeable, whatever happens!

Instructing:
- Before being given some jobs, people are required to have a medical check-up to make sure they are fit enough for what they are going to be doing. To check on our fitness for working in Jesus' Kingdom, we can go to "Doctor Jesus" (remember 5v31?) for an "I" test.

Seeing - Is there anything in my life that should not be there and is stopping me seeing properly what is right?

Speaking - How I talk shows what my "heart" is like. Am I overflowing with God's Word and Spirit in what I say?

Hearing - If I have been hearing properly then I will have been doing the things that Jesus has said to me.

• Jesus will not just tell us whether we pass or fail the test, he will do what a good doctor does - he will show us how to get better, and how to stay healthy!

28. 7v1-10 A soldier asks for Jesus' help

Informing:
• The Roman army made sure that the laws were obeyed in all the places that the Romans ruled, including the region called Palestine where Jesus lived. A centurion was a commander of a group of about 100 soldiers. They could be a mixture of men from different countries that Rome ruled, so we do not know where this centurion came from.
• Elders were community leaders who helped the Jews (the people of Israel) to obey God's laws.

Introducing:
• The centurion had heard enough about Jesus to know that he could and would heal people. Perhaps he had heard about Jesus healing the man in Capernaum who had been let down through the roof, when Jesus had said (5v24) that what he was doing showed that he had authority.
• Until this point people had been healed because they came or were brought to Jesus. Here the centurion asks Jesus to heal a person without meeting him.
• It must have been strange to be one of the people who were going with Jesus to see what he was going to do for the very ill person. Before he got there, Jesus stopped and let the man's friends go back to find him already healed!

Inspiring:
• The word that is used about the elders asking Jesus for help means that they called him alongside to help. This is the same word that Jesus used to describe the Holy Spirit (John 14v16) when he said that he would ask the Father and he would give them another one called alongside. Jesus says in that passage that when he himself is not with his followers, another helper like him will be there – the Holy Spirit – to make happen anything that could happen when Jesus was there. So Jesus still heals at a distance by the Holy Spirit being alongside us.

Instructing:

• There are people we would not expect to be interested, who are already open to God and who would be glad to be put in touch with Jesus. This "enemy" soldier of the occupying army loves the Jews, built them a place of worship, recognises that God's power is with Jesus, and that if Jesus gives the word, his servant will be healed!

• We do not know what experience had led him to love and respect the Jews, but we do know that he had faith because he had heard about Jesus. How many others might be healed if we make sure that people hear about Jesus, and if, like the centurion, we ask him to do it?

29. 7v11-17 Jesus raises a dead man

Informing:
• The funeral would not have been with a coffin as some Bibles say, but with the body covered with a cloth and carried on something like a stretcher that is used to carry injured people. The funeral would be taking place within a day of the person dying.
• Three groups of people meet at this funeral:
1) A group of disciples. They were people following Jesus to learn from him.
2) A group of others (called the crowd) who went with Jesus to see what he would do next.
3) The people from Nain, to whom Jesus was coming to bring the blessings of the Kingdom of heaven.

Introducing:
• We have seen what Jesus did for someone who was about to die; now we see what he does for someone who has just died!
• Jesus had compassion for the mother. The meaning of the word used for having compassion is when something affects you so strongly that you feel it in your stomach.
• Here Jesus was not answering a request for help; he decided to do what he did as an expression of his love.
• Here in his book, Luke begins to refer to Jesus as "the Lord" (as in v13 where he says that the Lord saw her). Before this, when Luke says, "the Lord", he is speaking about God, so when he uses the word about Jesus, we can see what he is saying about Jesus.
• The people say that Jesus is a great prophet. They mean someone who is able to say and do special things because he is in touch with God. They were probably thinking of him being like two Old Testament prophets, Elijah and Elisha who were both used by God to bring someone back to life. (1 Kings 17v17-24; 2 Kings 4v18-37)

Inspiring:
• If we trust the Holy Spirit to guide us in how we live, he will lead us to

be in exactly the right place at exactly the right time to be a blessing to others. The visit of Jesus to Nain came just at the right time for the widow, and for her son! Sometimes we might doubt the Holy Spirit's timing, but he never comes too soon, and he never comes too late, he always comes at the right time.

Instructing:

• The people said that God had come to his people, that is, he saw their need and was doing something about it. He looked out for them to look after them. What God did through Jesus and his compassion, he wants to do through us.

• In James 1v27 it says that if we are truly serving God, that will be seen in us looking out for the needs of widows and fatherless children. We may not be used to bring someone back to life for them (although it does happen!), but we can show them compassion in some way that the Holy Spirit will show us if we ask him.

30. 7v18-23 Jesus sends a message to John the Baptist

Informing:
- Why is John asking this question? There was a time when John the Baptist said clearly that Jesus was the special one that would come (John 1v30), and that Jesus was the Son of God (John 1v34). So this question is not saying that anything that Jesus was doing was not good, but rather it is John questioning whether <u>he</u> got it right in what <u>he</u> had thought and said about Jesus.
- John was in prison, and our feelings can be affected when we are going through a hard time. Also, John knew some things about the Messiah, but he did not know everything, so he became confused when Jesus did things in a way that was different from what he expected. John probably thought that the Messiah would get him out of prison and remove Herod!

Introducing:
- Here, Jesus is making it clear that he is the Messiah — God's specially chosen and anointed one. He is doing the things that the Messiah would do, so there is no good reason for anyone having a problem accepting him as being the Messiah. He was not doing everything that people thought that the Messiah would do, but he was doing what God had said the Messiah would do.
- They are amazing things which should make us very happy!

Inspiring:
- The Holy Spirit had said through the prophet Isaiah (Isaiah 35v5,6) that when God would come to his people, blind would see, deaf would hear, dumb would sing and lame would leap.
- God had told John (John 1v33) that the person upon whom the Holy Spirit came and stayed would be the special one from God.
- That had happened to Jesus, and Jesus said (Luke 4v18-19) that the Holy Spirit was upon him to do the things that the Messiah would do.
- Now by the power of the Holy Spirit, Jesus was doing all these things. So Jesus is reminding John that all these things fit together, so there is no

need for him to doubt – he had got it right. John could be happy knowing that he had done his job well!

Instructing:

• When, like John, we have doubts or questions, we should take them to Jesus. He will have an answer for us.

• Jesus wants us to be like the messengers, to say what we have seen and heard.

• If people question whether we are followers of Jesus, we should be able to say to them, "Look at how I am living and see what you think".

• Like John, there may be times when we feel down and wonder whether we have got things right. Those feelings don't mean that we have not done a good job. Many people who have served God have had doubts about themselves. We need to hear what Jesus says, what he says about himself, and about us.

31. 7v24-28 Jesus speaks about John the Baptist

Informing:
• When people talk of someone being greater than others, what is usually meant is that the person is in some way more important, has a higher rank or position, and should be treated in a special way. This is not what Jesus meant when he talked about someone being great. He explains his idea of greatness in Luke 22v24-27.
• The meaning that fits all the times when Jesus talks about someone being greater is, "someone who is able to do more".

Introducing:
• I think that Jesus must have had a smile on his face when he talked with people about John the Baptist.
• Was he like a blade of grass blowing in the wind, someone who would change what he says and does depending on what is happening around him? Certainly not! They knew he was not like that! John was determined, clear, challenging in what he said (see 3v7-20). That was why he had been put in prison.
• Was John a celebrity, a star dressed in fancy clothes and living in luxury? Certainly not! John was the opposite. He wore rough clothes of camel hair and animal skin and he ate locusts and wild honey!
• So what was he? Jesus wants them to know that John was even more than a prophet. They can be sure that John is the special messenger. By saying that, he is also making it clear that he, Jesus is the special one for whom John was preparing the way.

Inspiring:
• The Holy Spirit is upon different people in different ways at different times for the different work they are to do for the Kingdom of God:
The prophets spoke about the coming Kingdom.
John the Baptist got people ready for the coming Kingdom.
Jesus brought in the Kingdom.
We are now able to live and work in the power of the Kingdom.

Instructing:

• It is good and right to recognise and admire the special things that others have done in working for Jesus' Kingdom. But Jesus wants us to know that even if we think that we are the smallest or the youngest in his Kingdom, we are now able to do even more than John the Baptist because of what Jesus has done, and because the Holy Spirit is with us. If you think that what John did was great, you should see what God will call you to do with your life! You are special to Jesus, and you are special in his plans.

32. 7v29-35 Leaders reject what Jesus says

Informing:

• Have you ever found that others won't join in with what you are doing because it was not their idea and they don't like following someone else's lead? That is how Jesus is describing the Pharisees. It is as if they were children and someone is saying to them, "Let's play at weddings!" and they have said, "No, we don't feel like a singing and dancing game." So then it is suggested, "Let's play at funerals then, and we can pretend to be very sad and serious", and they have said, "No we don't want to do that either."

• They were saying about John the Baptist, "He is too serious; he can't be right", and then about Jesus, "He is too light-hearted; he can't be right!"

Introducing:

• Jesus came with God's purpose for everyone. He did not reject the Pharisees; they rejected him, and so missed God's purpose for their lives.

• Jesus was criticised for being "the friend of sinners", but that is a wonderfully true description of him. He is a friend to us. He is not the kind of friend who agrees with us when we do wrong or one who says that it does not matter, but a friend who helps us by freeing us from doing wrong.

Inspiring:

• When something is happening that we have not seen before, we may wonder if it is the work of the Holy Spirit. The test is not, "Do I like this way of doing things?" or "Who is it happening to?", but, "What is happening in the lives of the people who are involved?"

• Those who followed the wisdom of John, and then the wisdom of Jesus, showed by their changed lives that both John and Jesus were working with the Holy Spirit.

Instructing:

• God has some different ways of doing things, and some of his ways will surprise us. We are not in charge of the ways that God does things. He is! We must not get stuck in one way of God doing things; we should be ready for the change around from one way of doing things to another. Often, those who find it most difficult to accept a new way that God is working are those whom God has used in the special way that he was working before. John had been used by God but now wondered about the ways that Jesus was doing things. We should be like these tax collectors who received what God was doing through John, and went on to receive what God was doing through Jesus.

33. 7v36-50 A woman expresses her thanks to Jesus

Informing:
- At meals like this one, instead of using chairs, they lay on their side on big flat couches with their head towards the table and their feet towards the outside. It was usual before the meal to provide water to wash guests' feet. (Open sandals, bare feet and dusty roads made this a good idea.)
- Greeting a guest with a kiss showed that he was accepted as an equal, and perfumed water or oil was provided as an important part of making someone welcome.
- Alabaster is a soft stone used to make perfume bottles.

Introducing:
- Jesus knows what is going on in people's hearts.
- He knew what Simon was thinking and challenged him to see things more clearly and to change his attitude.
- Jesus knew what the woman was thinking, and he encouraged her in her steps of faith.
- He said to each of them what they needed to hear.

Inspiring:
- We see here the results of the Holy Spirit's work in this woman's life. She is here to do something for Jesus because of what he has already done for her. At some time before this, Jesus had said something to her, or done something for her which had let her know that she had been set free from her many sins.
- What she does in Simon's house is a big "Thank you" to Jesus. Her action is like a picture of someone when they are baptised as a follower of Jesus. The person has already experienced Jesus in a way which has changed their life on the inside, and now they openly show their thanks and their commitment to Jesus. That puts them in the place where the Holy Spirit can say more into their lives.

Instructing:
- We should be careful how we think about other people and what they

do. Simon looked like he was accepting and honouring Jesus by inviting him to a meal, but he was neither accepting Jesus nor honouring him. The woman did have a very bad past but what Simon did not know was that her life had been changed by Jesus.

• We should not criticise the way that someone else chooses to worship Jesus. While we may decide that we don't like what they are doing, Jesus may be deciding that he does not like what we are doing!

• It is good to ask Jesus to help us to see people as he sees them, and to thank him for all that he has done for us.

34. 8v1-3 A group of women travel with Jesus

Informing:
• There is important information here that on Jesus' journeys, he did not just have the 12 disciples with him. Along with some other men who went with them (mentioned in Acts 1v21,22), there was also a large group of women. We know from Luke 23v49 and 24v10 that these women went all the way to Jerusalem with him. Mary Magdalene was at the cross with Jesus' mother (John 19v25) and she was the first person to speak with Jesus after he came back alive (John 20v10-18).
• It is interesting to see from what Matthew wrote that at least two of the disciples, James and John had their mother along with them in the group that travelled with Jesus!

Introducing:
• In 4v43 Jesus said that he had to preach the Good News of the Kingdom of God to other towns because that is why he had been sent, so here we see him doing it. Two words are used to describe what he is doing; one means to announce, the other means to bring good news. So Jesus is not just teaching people about the Kingdom of God so that they can know things about it. He is announcing it, that is, telling people that it has come, and he is giving them the Good News that this Kingdom is for them, so that they can experience it for themselves.

Inspiring:
• The Holy Spirit puts together interesting groups of people for the work of Jesus' Kingdom. Here, there is someone (Mary) who used to be very much in the kingdom of darkness, someone (Joanna) whose husband worked for a ruler who was against God's Kingdom (Herod who put John the Baptist in prison), and someone who is unknown (Susanna – not mentioned anywhere else in the Bible), along with some other women who are happy to give their help by paying for what Jesus and his disciples need.

Instructing:

• We too can take part with others in serving Jesus.

• We can ask ourselves, "What have I got? Am I using it for Jesus?" We may not be as noticeable as some of Jesus' followers, but whatever Jesus has done in our lives is something that we can share with others, and whatever resources we have could be used to help in the work of his Kingdom. What could we give today?

35. 8v4-21 Jesus talks about God's Word in our lives

Informing:

• Telling parables is a way of teaching about us and God's Kingdom by using stories and pictures from ordinary life, and showing how lessons from these stories and pictures can help us to understand how God wants us to live.

• At first it seems strange to us that Jesus said that one result of him using parables would be that some people would not see or understand what he was talking about!

It also seems strange when he says later that people who don't have anything will have taken away from them what they think they have! When Jesus says those things he is not talking about people who want to know him and follow him. He is speaking about people who have already heard God speaking clearly to them and have then rejected what they have heard.

• A good thing about a parable is that even if, when a person hears it, they are not prepared to obey Jesus, they will still remember the story. This means that later, if they come to a point of being ready to listen to God, he can speak to them through the parable they were told before.

Introducing:

• Jesus' parable describes the different things that were happening in people as they heard him speaking God's Word to them. We can expect the same things to happen when we share God's message. Jesus wants his Word to come to us, to be in us and to come through us in the way we live.

• He makes it clear (v12) that there is an enemy who will do all that he can to stop that happening, but Jesus also speaks of great results in our lives when his Word is working in us.

Inspiring:

• When we are open to going God's way, the Holy Spirit will give us understanding of what he has to say to us.

• When we let Jesus do what he wants to do in our hearts, the Holy Spirit will let that be seen in our lives so that we will be like a lamp shining with Jesus' light.

• When we give our lives to Jesus, the Holy Spirit makes us one of his family and helps us to grow to be more and more like him.

Instructing:

• The very clear instruction in verse 18 is that we should watch and take care of how we listen to what God is saying to us, so that we can receive all that he is giving to us.

To make sure that we allow that to happen, Jesus' parable points out four things that can help us:

1) We should decide to shut the Devil out of our lives.

2) We should decide that we will not give up when things get tough.

3) We should decide that we will keep clear of being wrongly affected by worries, riches or pleasure.

4) We should decide to keep living in the way that Jesus has shown us.

36. 8v22-39 Jesus brings peace

Informing:

• "The abyss" or "the deep" (v31) that the demons begged Jesus not to send them to, is the opposite of heaven. We might think that evil spirits would want to be there, but it is not a place of freedom for evil, but a place of containing and imprisoning it.

Introducing:

• There is always more of Jesus for us to experience. The disciples thought they knew him well, but when they see him order the winds and the waves to be calm, they wonder who he is that can do such a thing.

• The man, whose evil spirit storm inside him was calmed by Jesus, seems to have known who Jesus is. When Jesus tells him to go back home and tell what God has done for him, he goes through the whole town telling what Jesus had done for him.

• We see in these events Jesus as very human and very divine:

Very human – in the boat he was tired and fell asleep.

Very divine – he was able to change the behaviour of winds, waves and a crowd of evil sprits, and was recognised by them as the Son of the Most High God.

Inspiring:

• This was a wonderful Holy Spirit arranged meeting. Here was a man who, humanly speaking, was totally uncontrollable, yet at the point when Jesus steps out of the boat, he is right there meeting him! We are not told the story of this man's life, how and why he allowed his life to be taken over by evil spirits, but how much God must have loved him! The Holy Spirit directed Jesus to be there just for him to set him free.

• Holy Spirit power is more than enough for any storm in life, whether, wind, waves or evil spirits. The Holy Spirit brings peace.

Instructing:

• Are we ready for the unexpected things that Jesus may have for us?

• He took his disciples into a storm and it was a frightening experience for them. But Jesus did not just take them <u>into</u> the storm, he was with them <u>in</u> the storm, and he took them <u>through</u> and <u>past</u> the storm.

• The man wanted to go with Jesus. That was a good thing to want, but Jesus said, "No" and gave him somewhere else to be, and something else to do which only he could do.

• Whatever Jesus decides is the best for us.

• If we are asked the question, "Where is your faith?" our answer can be that we trust the love of Jesus and the power of the Holy Spirit for everything that we face each day.

37. 8v40-56 Jesus' touch brings healing

Informing:

• The demonized man had fallen down before Jesus and now so does Jairus, and the woman who is healed. To go down on the ground in front of someone is a way of saying, "You are greater than I am, and I am looking to your greatness to help me in my need."

• Jesus had just left a place where people did not want him, and comes to be in touch with others who were looking for him and were waiting for him. Although it can be hurtful when people reject us, it can leave us free to be spending time with those who are more open to Jesus.

Introducing:

• Jesus sees things in a way that is different from others.

• The disciples saw a crowd pressing in on Jesus; he noticed that someone had touched him.

• The people at Jairus' house said that the girl was dead; Jesus saw her as "asleep".

• Jesus saw that the woman would be helped by her story being made public, and he saw that the girl would be helped by her story being kept private.

• While the girl's parents were astonished at her coming back to life, Jesus knew that she would be hungry and needed something to eat!

Inspiring:

• Here is perfect timing from the Holy Spirit again. If Jesus had stayed longer on the other side of the lake, the girl would have been dead and buried. Jairus was probably frantic at the delay caused by the crowds and then Jesus taking time to help the woman, but even when it looks too late, the Holy Spirit has not got it wrong. He wants to show Jesus doing something even more special.

• The woman that Jesus healed here is the only person that we read of that he addressed as "Daughter". At other times he says, "Woman". We don't know why he spoke to her in this way, but there will have been a special Holy Spirit reason for it.

Perhaps she was a young woman. Perhaps she needed to hear a word that treated her as one of the family. Perhaps with Jairus concerned only about <u>his</u> daughter, he needed to see that this woman was as precious to Jesus as the one who was so precious to him.

Instructing:
• The clear lesson here is what Jesus said to Jairus when he told him that all he had to do was believe. What does that mean?

• Jesus said that the woman had believed – she had faith. She knew that Jesus had healing power, so she reached out to be in touch with that power for her own need.

Just as Jairus saw the results in this woman's life of her trusting Jesus, so we can see the results in other people's lives when they are trusting Jesus. Then, the challenge comes to us as it did to Jairus – now <u>you</u> believe! For Jairus, that meant not giving up on Jesus, but instead, letting him in to do what he wanted to do.

• So let us "believe" – reach out for Jesus' power in our lives, and let him in to do what he wants to do.

38. 9v1-9 The disciples go on a mission

Informing:
- Luke mentions in 3v20 that Herod had put John the Baptist in prison. Here Herod speaks about having had John killed. The story of how this happened is in Matthew 14v1-12.
- In the last book of the Old Testament, Malachi prophesied that an Elijah would be sent to prepare for the Messiah (Malachi 4v5). In Luke 1v17 the angel said that John the Baptist would be like Elijah.

Introducing:
- Herod asked the big question about Jesus, "Who is this?"
- There is obviously something special about someone who can heal people and set them free from evil spirits. There has to be something extra-special about someone who can pass on to others the power to do those things. Here Jesus shows how he is going to work, by working through his followers.
- He calls them, he gives them what they need, he sends them out to speak and to do things, and he gives special instructions for each mission. He gives them <u>authority</u> – the right to do it, and <u>power</u> – the ability to make it happen.

Inspiring:
- The power of the Holy Spirit is given for the work of Jesus' Kingdom. It is a power that can heal, and can overcome <u>all</u> evil spirits, and can bring people to recognise and receive Jesus as their King. The Kingdom is offered to people, not forced on them. They are free to refuse it, but they need to know that it is an important decision.
- Shaking dust off your feet is like saying, "We have offered you something pure that would make this a clean place, but you have said no, and you are choosing uncleanness. We don't want any of that uncleanness on us because we are committed to a pure clean kingdom."

Instructing:
- The instructions that Jesus gave about what to take and what not to

take were for <u>this</u> mission. At other times he would give different instructions. (See 22v35-36)

• Here he is giving the 12 the opportunity to experience the truth of his words in 12v29-31, when he says that there is no need for them to be worried about food and drink as their heavenly Father knows their needs and will provide for them if they concern themselves with his Kingdom.

• Also, they were to rely on people receiving them, so they did not have resources of their own to use for spending time with people who did not want what they had to say.

• There are people who are ready to receive what Jesus wants to give to them through us. It is important that we find them, rather than wasting time arguing with others who do not (at this point) want to say yes to Jesus' Kingdom.

39. 9v10-17 Jesus feeds a crowd

Informing:
    • This event is also written about in the other 3 books about Jesus (Matthew 14v13-21; Mark 6v31-44; John 6v1-13). There are different parts of the story that each one tells. Mark tells that Jesus was taking his disciples away to rest because before this, they had been so busy they had not even had time to eat. John tells us about the boy who had the bread and the fish.

Introducing:
    We see here what Jesus' love leads him to do.
    • He welcomes and receives all who come to him. (In John 6v37 Jesus says he will never turn away anyone who comes to him.)
    • He teaches us how to live in God's Kingdom.
    • He heals people, whatever their particular need is.
    • He uses his followers as his partners in his work.
    • He puts people into togetherness with one another. (He made them sit to eat in groups of 50.)
    • He does amazing things with what is given to him.
    • He provides enough for everyone to be completely satisfied.

Inspiring:
    • The things that happened with this big crowd are like the special Holy Spirit times that are called "revival" – times when large numbers of people become hungry for God because of what Jesus has begun to do in their area.
    • These people came running out of their towns along the coast, chasing Jesus and his disciples who were in a boat!
    • They stayed longer than was normal. It was getting dark, they had not eaten, and they did not leave until Jesus told them to go.
    • They experienced supernatural miraculous power and went away completely satisfied. The Holy Spirit still works in this way today and it can be nearer than we think. The disciples had said that they were in a desert place, and then, in the next hour, more than 5000 people were being fed!

Instructing:

There are lessons here in working together with Jesus.

• He wants us to have times of rest, but sometimes we will have to give up our time off to help others.

• Working with Jesus does not mean us telling Jesus what to do (like the disciples tried to do in v12) but rather, Jesus telling us what to do, and us doing it, with Jesus doing what we can't do.

• With Jesus, we are only one prayer away from a miracle.

• We may not have very much (like the bread and fish), but if we give what we have to Jesus, he can do things that we cannot do by ourselves.

40. 9v18-27 Jesus explains what knowing him means

Informing:
- People saying that Jesus might be John, Elijah or another prophet raised from the dead shows that they believed that such things might happen, and that they recognised something special from God in Jesus.
- The Elders, Chief Priests and Teachers of the Law were the religious leaders of the Jews. They did go on to do what Jesus said here that they would do.
- Jesus as Messiah - see *Introducing:* 10. 2v21-40
- Jesus as Son of Man - see *Introducing:* 21. 5v17-26
- People being crucified would be made to carry their cross to the place where they would be nailed to it.

Introducing:
- In telling what is going to happen to him, Jesus shows that he is choosing to go to his death, and that what is going to happen will all be used in God's plan.
- When Jesus says here not to be ashamed of him, it might seem strange for him to be saying at the same time that they must not tell people that he is the Messiah. He said this because people had wrong expectations of what the Messiah would do. They expected him to be like a political or government leader. People who liked him would (as Peter did) want things to be different from the way that Jesus was going to go. They, and those who were against Jesus, might then do things which would get in the way of God's plan. It was best for them not to know until the special work of the Messiah had been done, and then everyone could be told.

Inspiring:
- Special things can come from times spent in prayer as happened here. The Holy Spirit can bring to Jesus' followers what they need to know to be prepared for what is to come.
- The Kingdom of God which Jesus brought was going to be sent out throughout the world in power after Jesus had died, risen again and sent the Holy Spirit on the day of Pentecost which Luke describes in his second

book, Acts in chapter 2. (Not all who heard Jesus here would be alive then. Judas, who betrayed him, would be dead by then.)

• The Holy Spirit brings glory out of suffering, and the power of the Kingdom out of lives that are given away in serving Jesus.

Instructing:

• It takes time to understand properly who Jesus is and to understand his ways of working.

• Jesus wants us as his followers to be ready to live for him, and if necessary to die for him, knowing that we will not lose out by doing so.

• Accepting Jesus' ways of doing things rather than our own involves being ready to face being rejected, even by people we would have expected to accept us. It also means being proud of Jesus and not ashamed to belong to him, whatever happens, looking for Jesus' Kingdom and his glory (that is when Jesus' specialness is revealed and seen), and deciding each day to live for Jesus.

41. 9v28-36 Jesus has a special meeting on a mountain

Informing:

• The teaching and the time of the Old Testament were sometimes described as "the Law and the Prophets". Moses was a main person of "the Law" and Elijah was a main person of "the Prophets".

• Peter's idea of tents could have come from remembering about the special tent that Moses had on the journey of the Israelites through the desert. At that tent God spoke to Moses face to face in the way that someone speaks to a friend and there was a special cloud showing that God was there. (Exodus 33v 10,11)

• The disciples were asleep for some of the time and we do not know how long this special meeting lasted. Jesus and the disciples did not go down from the mountain until the next day.

Introducing:

• Peter had said before this that some people thought that Jesus might be an Old Testament prophet who had come back to life. Here he sees Jesus alongside two of them and Jesus is shown to be more important than they are.

• There is always more to Jesus than we have seen so far, even when we know him well. Peter, James and John were close friends of Jesus, but this was the first time they had seen him appear in this very special way.

• The special conversation was about the greatest part of God's special plan. Moses had been part of that plan, and then Elijah had been too. Now they were with Jesus when he was about to do the greatest thing in God's plan by dying on the cross to make the way for us to be brought into a right togetherness with God.

Inspiring:

• This very special experience for Peter, James and John was like the door of heaven being opened to them – with Jesus standing in the doorway shining with his heavenly brightness, Elijah and Moses seen to be alive in heaven, and God's nearness being seen and felt and his voice clearly heard.

• We never know how much may happen when a few of us spend some time praying together with Jesus!

Instructing:

• The Holy Spirit may give us special experiences. When that happens it is important that we do not do the wrong thing with what has happened. We might be excited like Peter, thinking that we must do something straight away, when God wants us instead to listen more to Jesus.

• Along with being willing to speak at the right time about what God has shown us, we will be sometimes be shown things that are particularly for ourselves, to help us, to change us and to prepare us for what God wants to do through us. We are meant to keep quiet about some things like this. There may be a time later, like there was for these disciples, when it will be right to tell others about it to help them too.

42. 9v37-45 A boy is set free from an evil spirit

Informing:

Why did Jesus say that he was speaking to a generation that was unbelieving and twisted?

• Firstly it applies to the people of that place and time who lived in such a way that led to children being affected by evil spirits. This could include the boy's father who may have been responsible for his son getting into this condition.

• It applies too to the disciples. When they asked Jesus why they could not overcome this evil spirit, Jesus told them that it was because they had so little faith, which they could increase by prayer and fasting (see Matthew 17v14-21).

• It applies also to the teachers of the law that Mark mentions who were arguing with the disciples about the disciples failing to bring healing to the boy. (See Mark 9v14-29.)

Introducing:

• On the mountain on the day before this event, Jesus' glory (his specialness) was seen "at the door of heaven". Here his glory is seen "at the door of hell" as he frees this boy from the strong hold that the evil spirit had over his life and which no one else had been able to overcome.

• After healing the boy, Jesus once again tells his disciples about his coming suffering. He wants to warn them in advance that, since he has the power to overcome all evil, what is going to happen to him is because he has decided to let it happen.

Inspiring:

• What wonderful Holy Spirit timing happens here! Jesus arrives at the perfect time for the man who has just had the disappointment of the disciples not being able to help.

• It is also the perfect time for the disciples who would be feeling disappointed at not being able to drive out this evil spirit when they had overcome other evil spirits before.

• It was most importantly the perfect time for the boy, who in meeting Jesus was set completely free and was totally healed.

Instructing:

• In asking how long he should stay with them and put up with them, Jesus is not annoyed at the bringing of the boy to him for healing.

• Matthew tells us (Matthew 17v20-21) that afterwards Jesus told his disciples that with even a little faith <u>they</u> would be able to move big obstacles. So Jesus was, and is, looking for his followers to be able to take care of situations like this one where powerful forces of evil are at work. Jesus wants us not just to believe in his power, but to believe in his power working through us.

• When, like the disciples experienced, it does not seem to work, let us not give up. Instead we should go back to Jesus to see what he wants to say and do. Nothing is beyond his power.

43. 9v46-62 Jesus answers questions

Informing:
• People in Samaria disagreed with the Jews. They had their own ways, beliefs and a place to worship instead of Jerusalem. Like the Jews they were looking for the Messiah to come, so perhaps, if they had known who Jesus was and why he was going to Jerusalem, they might not have rejected him.
• James and John's idea of calling down fire from heaven came from a time in the Old Testament when Elijah did that in Samaria. (2 Kings 1)
• Looking forward when ploughing is the way to make sure that the ploughing is done properly in a straight line.

Introducing:
• Jesus' focus is on the work of the Kingdom of God.
• Knowing what he has to do, Jesus is determined to go to Jerusalem to do it. He expects determination in his followers:
1) not to say we will follow then give up at the times when it is uncomfortable.
2) not to be turned away from Jesus' call by what godless people (whom Jesus describes as "the dead") expect of us.
3) not to fit our commitment to Jesus into our family life, but to fit our family life into our commitment to Jesus' Kingdom, always putting him first.
• Jesus knows their thoughts. That is why he was able to give exactly the right answers to the different people he was speaking to.

Inspiring:
• There are many different writings in the original language (called manuscripts) which are used when translating the New Testament into English. Where a verse is in some manuscripts but not in others, this is shown in some Bibles at the bottom of the page, as in verse 55 where Jesus challenges his disciples about their attitude being different from his. Our living for Jesus' Kingdom must be done in a Holy Spirit way.
• Later the disciples had the opportunity to bring a different kind of "fire"

down in Samaria. Acts 8v14-17 says that when the apostles heard that people in Samaria were accepting God's Word, they sent Peter and John to them, and when Peter and John placed their hands on them, they received the Holy Spirit.

Instructing:

• When Jesus used a child to teach the disciples, he was showing that the greatest thing in the work of his Kingdom is to have Jesus with us and to bring him to others. We can do that whatever age we are.

• In being keen to live for Jesus it is important to be careful not to do and say things that are <u>our</u> ways and <u>our</u> words, but to ask the Holy Spirit to show us what we need to know, so that we say and do things as <u>he</u> wants.

44. 10v1-16 Seventy two go on a mission

Informing:

• Sodom was a town in the Old Testament which was destroyed by God because of its great wickedness (Genesis 19; Ezekiel 16v49,50). Tyre and Sidon were cities which in Old Testament times had badly treated their neighbours, the people of Israel. Chorazin and Bethsaida were towns where Jesus had done many miracles, as was Capernaum where Jesus had been based for some time.

• In mentioning "that day" and "the judgement", Jesus is pointing to the time when God will judge people on the basis of what they have experienced of his Kingdom and how they have responded to that.

• The instructions about eating were because they might be offered food which had been part of sacrifices to idols, or were foods which Jews did not usually eat. They were not to let such things stop them from accepting someone's hospitality.

Introducing:

• Luke begins this chapter referring to Jesus as "the Lord" as he does in several places. (see *Introducing:* 29. 7v11-17.)

• When Jesus tells of a great harvest, he means people being brought to know God and to live as his family. He wants that to happen through the partnership of people who already know him sharing with others his love and his power.

• In sending out this new big group on this mission, Jesus shows that the things that he expected the 12 disciples to do were not just for them as a special group, but for any of his followers who are working to bring his Kingdom to others.

Inspiring:

Whenever we go for Jesus to bring his Kingdom to others, he wants us to do that in:

• a spirit of gentleness – being like lambs even when others around are like wolves.

• a spirit of trust – expecting God to protect and provide.

• a spirit of single-mindedness – not letting anything divert us from the purpose of the mission.

• a spirit of peace – bringing Jesus' peace to those who will receive it, and not losing our peace when we are rejected.

• a spirit of contentment – being satisfied and accepting what is given to us.

• a spirit of healing – looking to bless people with the power of God.

• a spirit of boldness – not being afraid to warn people about the danger of rejecting Jesus.

• a spirit of expectation – knowing that, though some will reject, there will be those who will gladly accept what we bring of Jesus to them.

Instructing:

• Jesus wants us to be aware of, and to care about the many people who do not yet know him. He wants to get us praying about them being reached for Jesus' Kingdom, and to get us ready to be appointed by him to take part in that work – to be shown when, where and how we can work with Jesus and with others in introducing people to him.

45. 10v17-24 Jesus speaks about the mission

Informing:
- The demons (evil spirits) which had been more powerful than the people whose lives they had been spoiling, had less power than these ordinary people working and speaking for Jesus on this mission. This could be pictured as these evil spirit powers going from <u>above</u> people to being <u>below</u> them. Jesus said that this showed Satan's entire rule was going from a place of power to a place of being overcome.
- Satan is described in other parts of the Bible as "the Snake", so treading on snakes and scorpions is a picture of overcoming evil spirits which people may have been afraid of before.

Introducing:
- Although Luke has written before about Jesus praying, this is the first time we have words that Jesus said when he was praying. It is a joyful prayer, showing that it makes Jesus, the Father and the Holy Spirit really happy when good things are happening in and through ordinary people.
- Getting to know Jesus and Father as they really are, and being involved in the work of Jesus' Kingdom, do not happen by people being clever or religious, or by them working things out by their own efforts or understanding. They happen because Jesus uncovers it all to us; he shows us everything that we need to know. What he hides from proud people who think they are clever, he shows to humble people, the kind of people that others think would not be able to understand.

Inspiring:
- More can be happening through ordinary people, working in the power of the Holy Spirit, than they can see themselves. The people on this mission saw what happened to the people and the demons they were dealing with. Jesus saw what was happening as part of the bigger picture of victory over Satan, and as part of overcoming Satan's work.

Instructing:
- It is good to look for opportunities to be involved in special activities

working for Jesus with others.

• It is a way of making people happy by bringing to them Jesus' love and power.

• It is a way of making ourselves happy when we see what Jesus will do through us.

• Best of all it is a way of making Jesus, Father and the Holy Spirit happy.

• Whatever the excitement and special experiences of such times, Jesus wants us to be most happy that our names are written in heaven. God recognises us, accepts us and has a special place for us. We are not to rejoice about us being "above" other powers, but to rejoice in what is "above" us, that is Jesus and his heavenly Kingdom.

So nothing will harm us, nothing will deny us our rights or have authority over us.

46. 10v25-37 Jesus tells a story about loving your neighbour

Informing:

• This expert in Jewish law has a good question – how can he be in a right relationship with God and be accepted in heaven when he dies? He comes to the right person with that question. He also has a good knowledge of God's Word. Jesus agrees with his answer. But he is trying to test Jesus rather than to receive what Jesus has to say. He wants to show himself to be right, so when he asks who is his neighbour, he is asking, "What is it about a person that means they are someone I must love?" In others words, "Who do I not have to love?" It would have been better if instead he had said, "Even though I know it is right to love God and my neighbour, I have failed to live in that way. Can I be forgiven, and be given the power to live that way?"

• The man would have believed that Samaritans were wrong in their beliefs and practices and that they would not be among those who would receive eternal life. John in his book says that Jews did not associate with Samaritans (John 4v9), and in rejecting Jesus (John 8v48), Jews said that they did so because they accused him of being a Samaritan and having a demon.

• The Levites were the tribe of Israel who took care of worship at the temple in Jerusalem. The priest would be one of those who took part in the worship services. The Levite would be one of those who worked in the temple organisation.

• Wine was good for the wounds because the alcohol in it is an antiseptic which can kill germs. Olive oil is good for soothing injuries and helping to heal them.

Introducing:

• Whenever people put Jesus to the test, he always had a perfect and surprising answer for them, as he had in this unforgettable story.

• In the story Jesus indicates that it is possible to be involved in religious work (Levite) or even be taking part in worship services (priest) and still miss what God expects of us. He shows that love is not a matter of following closely a set of rules and laws, but having a heart of compassion and mercy, really caring for the feelings and needs of other people (whoever they are) and doing all we can to help.

• Have you noticed how much the Samaritan in the story is like Jesus?

Inspiring:

• The Holy Spirit can provide the exact right answer for each person's question. Jesus was asked exactly the same question by someone else later (18v18) but he gave that person a different answer which fitted him. Let us not be like the expert in the law who thought he knew the right answers, but rather, let us learn to rely on the Holy Spirit for each occasion.

Instructing:

• Let us be careful not to just see this story as a wonderful answer to this man, and miss the message to us to go and be like the Samaritan in the things that we do.

• And let us remember, the most unlikely people might be closer to God than we think! The expert in the Jewish law would not have expected a Samaritan to be used as an example of someone living as God wants.

47. 10v38-41 Jesus visits Martha and Mary

Informing:
• Martha welcomed Jesus into her home. This would have meant quite a lot of work as he had his 12 disciples with him, and there may have been others too who wanted to see him. Martha expected Mary to be helping with the housework and was annoyed when she found that Mary was listening to Jesus instead.

• Jesus said that Martha was worried and upset about many things, probably including: preparing a meal for at least 15 people, organising where they would all sleep and finding some time to be with Jesus.

• Martha could have decided to join Mary while Jesus was talking, and leave the other arrangements until afterwards (when Mary would have been available).

• She could have decided to leave Mary to enjoy spending time with Jesus, and to happily look after all the preparation work herself, without feeling the need to do more than she could manage on her own.

Introducing:
• Jesus does not want serving him to become a difficult burden for us to carry. It is important to Jesus that we are able to spend time with him, enjoying his company and hearing what he has to say to us.

• Jesus is not correcting Martha for doing her work instead of being with him. He is correcting her for getting agitated about the things she thought she had to do.

• When Martha complained to Jesus, Mary might well have been embarrassed and thought, "Oh well, maybe I had better go and help her", but Jesus gives a strong "No!" to that. He confirms that she has chosen well and that nothing should take that away from her.

Inspiring:
• Often in our lives it will seem that there are many things that we could be doing. At any time, God only expects us to be in one place doing one thing. Only one thing is needed. We cannot be more effective or pleasing to God by being anywhere else and doing anything else, however big or

important it may look.

• The Holy Spirit will guide us in how to be in the right place at the right time, doing the right thing in the right way. He will also give us peace about the things that we are not able to do.

• If we are not at peace about what we are doing in serving Jesus, it could be because we are doing things that the Holy Spirit has not asked us to do.

Instructing:

• Sometimes in wanting to serve Jesus we can try to do more than we should. Rather than getting upset or trying to do everything at once, we should look for the best thing to do at that point.

• It is not our place to criticise others for the way in which they spend their time, especially when they are spending time for Jesus. If we have the privilege of doing serving, preparation, background work like Martha, we should be glad to be allowing others to be hearing from Jesus, and recognise that what we are doing is valued too.

48. 11v1-13 Jesus teaches about prayer

Informing:
- Jesus teaches his followers to put God and his ways first in everything, and to look to him for provision, forgiveness, guidance and protection.
- The stories help us to know that God is more ready to help us than a best friend, and more loving than the best father.
- The house in the story would have had only one room for all the family to sleep in, so getting up would mean disturbing them all.
- Jesus had already used the idea of snakes and scorpions as pictures of evil things that come from the Devil, things which God is opposed to. (10v19)
- It is interesting to see that Jesus, in talking to the disciples mentions that some of them are fathers (v11), so some of them would have had a wife and children to care for at the same time as they were travelling and working with Jesus.

Introducing:
- Jesus gives this teaching about prayer when he is asked to give it. Sometimes he waits until we want something enough to ask for it.
- The disciples had heard Jesus pray, and they had heard him talk to God as "Father" (10v21). They knew that <u>Jesus</u> had a special relationship with God, and here, Jesus tells them that <u>they too</u> can speak to God as <u>their</u> Father. We can sometimes be so used to this, that we miss the amazing, special privilege that Jesus brought to us of being able to know God in this way.
- Another amazing statement that Jesus makes here is that <u>everyone</u> who asks will receive. There is something good for everyone who looks to him.

Inspiring:
- Jesus ends this part of teaching by speaking about the Father giving the Holy Spirit to those who ask him, but before this, in teaching about prayer, he has not said that we should ask for the Holy Spirit. Why? Perhaps because all of prayer is meant to be a way of putting us in touch

with the Holy Spirit, to receive him, and let his power flow through us.
  • How do we know God as Father? By the Holy Spirit.
  • How does his Kingdom come? By the power of the Holy Spirit.
  • What do we need from God day by day? The Holy Spirit.
  • How do we experience forgiveness in us and through us? By the Holy Spirit.
  • How are we guided and protected? By the Holy Spirit.
  • When we are looking for what God wants in our lives, we have no reason to be afraid of what the Holy Spirit will bring to us.

Instructing:
  • If we want to learn more from Jesus, we can ask him. Father wants us to keep coming, asking, looking, and knocking.
  • We must not miss that if we want God's forgiveness, we must also allow forgiveness to flow through us to others.
  • Notice that the story about asking, seeking and knocking is to get what is needed for <u>someone else</u> (food for a friend). Along with asking God for what we need, let us be always asking him for what is needed to bless others.

49. 11v14-28 Jesus teaches about overcoming Satan

Informing:
- Evil spirits do different things to harm people. Here, this one made the man unable to talk. The man in 4v33 was made to scream, the man in 8v29 was uncontrollable, and the boy in 9v39 was made unwell and injured.
- Beelzebul was a local name used for Satan.
- In speaking about gathering and scattering, Jesus is using the picture of himself as a shepherd <u>gathering</u> a flock of sheep. In John 10v12 Jesus speaks of the flock being attacked and the wolf <u>scattering</u> the sheep.

Introducing:
- In v17 Jesus is saying that since freeing the man from the evil spirit would weaken Satan's kingdom, how could they suggest that he was serving Satan by doing it?
- In v19 Jesus mentions that there are those amongst them who try to help people to be free from evil spirits, so if they are accusing him of doing wrong, they are accusing their own people too.
- In v21-22, in explaining which kingdom is being served by what he is doing, Jesus describes himself as a "stronger man", stronger than the "strong man", Satan. Jesus has been able to free the man from Satan's grip and has given him back what Satan had stolen from him, his power to speak.

Inspiring:
- What a shame that when people were questioning Jesus, they were missing the wonderful fact that a man who had been unable to speak was now speaking, and that God was touching the place where they were. Holy Spirit power was at work through Jesus to defeat Satan's hold over people's lives and to bring the freedom of God's Kingdom.
- When the Holy Spirit is at work, it always brings a choice to people who see it. They will either recognise it and accept it, or they will oppose it and reject it.

Instructing:

• We should remember that whatever power of evil we come up against, Jesus is stronger.

• We are to help people not only to stop making room for evil in their lives, but to help them to make room for the Holy Spirit to fill their lives.

• Jesus wants us to be helpers in "gathering a flock", bringing people to know him as their shepherd and to follow him together.

• As Jesus said to the woman, he wants us not just to admire what he does, but to be part of what he is doing by living in obedience to what God says.

• It is a happy adventure working for God's Kingdom in the power of the Holy Spirit, seeing people's lives changed by Jesus!

50. 11v29-36 Jesus challenges people to see clearly

Informing:

• For the story of Jonah and Nineveh, see the book of Jonah in the Old Testament.

• For the story of the Queen and Solomon, see 1 Kings 10 or 2 Chronicles 9.

• Some people had been asking Jesus to give a miraculous sign to show that what he said and did were from God (v16) but Jesus showed that such signs are not needed; his words and actions were clear enough.

• The people of Nineveh were able to recognise Jonah's message as being from God and they repented (turned from their evil). The Queen of Sheba /the South/ Ethiopia was able to recognise that Solomon's wisdom came from God and she received it. If these people from ungodly countries could recognise God's Word, the Jews should have easily recognised God's message coming to them through Jesus.

• Jesus speaks of "the judgement", a time when people from every age who have died will be brought to life again and will be judged for how they have responded to what they have heard of God's Word.

Introducing:

• Jesus had something greater than Solomon had. Solomon had some of God's wisdom, but Jesus has all of God's wisdom. Jesus had something greater than Jonah had. Jonah had God's message for a particular people at one time, but Jesus has God's message for everyone at all times.

• To understand what Jesus says about the eye as a light for the body, it is helpful to think about a camera lens as a light for the camera. If a camera takes a photograph of a bright sunrise, and the picture turns out dark, that shows that the lens of the camera must be dirty, not that there is anything wrong with the sunrise! If someone looks at Jesus and does not see him as good and true, there is something evil in them that needs to change.

• As Jesus said, the people of his time were given a sign like Jonah. Just as Jonah was three days in the fish then alive again, so Jesus would be three days in the ground then be alive again.

Inspiring:

• If we want our lives to be full of light (truth and goodness), then we need a light to be shining in us. That light is the Holy Spirit who helps us to see things as they really are. His light will shine when, like the people of Nineveh, we turn away from what displeases God, and when, like the Queen of Sheba, we accept God's Word.

Instructing:

• Jesus warns us to beware of thinking like the people of our generation, or following what the crowd thinks. We should pay attention to the wisdom we can get from God's Written Word, the Bible. We should pay attention to God's Prophetic Word, his message to us at a particular time, and we should pay attention to God's Living Word, Jesus - all he is, says and does. If we do that, we will be full of light, shining brightly for others to see Jesus in us, so that they might be like the Queen of Sheba who said (2 Chronicles 9v5,6) that she had heard but she did not believe until she came and she saw for herself.

51. 11v37-54 Jesus has strong words for Pharisees

Informing:

• The Pharisees and Teachers of the Law - see *Informing:* 21. 5v17-26.

• Dipping hands in water before a meal was meant to show that the person was being made clean from having been in contact with non-religious people or things during that day.

• "Tithing", giving a tenth of each year's crops or income, was something that God required the Israelites to do, in order to supply what was needed for festivals, to support the work of the priests and the Levites, and to help the poor.

Introducing:

• This incident shows some of the harshest words that Jesus ever said. The reason that Jesus was being so strong in what he said to these people was that they were falsely claiming to be representing God's Kingdom, when much of what they did was very far away from God's ways. Jesus criticised them for:

1) Bothering about how their contact with other people might affect themselves (being made unclean) rather than how their contact with other people could bring blessing to those people (giving to the poor).

2) Being very religious about small things (tithing herbs) while not giving attention to big important things (justice and loving God).

3) Wanting to be respected and treated as special (best seats in the synagogue), when they had done no good that they would be remembered for after they died (like unmarked graves).

4) Making up lots of rules for people's lives while failing to help them live God's way.

5) Making a show of respecting the prophets, while rejecting their teaching.

6) Misusing God's "key" - his Word (at that time, the Old Testament), so that they and those they taught were prevented from understanding its true meaning.

• Jesus prophesied God's judgement on that generation. They were being given the fullness of what God had to say in Jesus, and in what the apostles would say about him. By rejecting this, they were also rejecting all the Old Testament prophets and their teaching, so they were guilty like those who had killed them.

Inspiring:

• The Holy Spirit is <u>very</u> different from the spirit of the Pharisees and the Teachers of the Law. Being led by the Holy Spirit will make us generous, committed to what is right, loving, humble, supportive, open to what God is saying, and open to sharing that freely with others.

Instructing:

• This is the second of 3 times that Luke tells of Jesus having a meal with a Pharisee (7v36, 11v37, 14v1). Jesus shows that we can and should be willing to spend time with people whose views are different from ours, but we should not change our values to suit them. We should be ready, where it is right to do so, to challenge them about what they say and do.

• A lesson from the Pharisee's experience is that if we invite Jesus to come, we should be ready to receive whatever he wants to say and do.

52. 12v1-12 Jesus warns and encourages

Informing:
- Yeast is the very small ingredient which, when mixed with flour and water, makes that dough rise to become bread. It is unnoticeable at first, but afterwards its effects seen clearly. Some of the things which the Pharisees said and did were not noticeably bad at first but became clear later.
- Jesus speaks of life beyond death, a place with the angels of God - heaven, and a place of judgement - hell. The word used for hell is "Gehenna" which was the name of a continually burning rubbish dump outside Jerusalem.
- Along with knowing how many hairs we have, there is another way in which our hairs are "numbered" by God. It is now possible for scientists, by examining just one hair, to know that it comes from a particular person and no one else because every hair contains our unique DNA code or number. Each of our hairs has a "number" which is different from everyone else's.

Introducing:
- Jesus, in speaking about his place in heaven, shows that it belongs to him. He is the one who is going to say whether or not a person is one of his and has a right to be there.
- Although Jesus had a great love for the crowds who came to him, he did not let them decide what he was going to do. Here, even though there is a huge crowd, Jesus decides to speak first to his disciples.
- Jesus has a lovely way of speaking to his followers; he speaks of them as his friends.

Inspiring:
- When Jesus says that this speaking against the Holy Spirit will not be forgiven, he is not saying that there is a sin so bad that it cannot be forgiven. There are many people who have been very opposed to the work of the Holy Spirit who have then changed and become followers of Jesus. It is rather that when people set themselves against what the Holy Spirit is

saying to them and doing with them, they are setting themselves against God's love and friendship. By doing that, <u>they</u> <u>are</u> <u>choosing</u> not to receive his forgiveness.

• There is no way for people to be put right with God by their own efforts as the Pharisees were teaching. If people are like the Pharisees and refuse the truth about Jesus that the Holy Spirit brings to them, they are refusing the experience of forgiveness that is being offered to them.

Instructing:
• Are we committed to Father? He is committed to caring for us. (v7)
• Are we committed to Jesus? He is committed to us, giving us our place in heaven. (v8)
• Are we committed to the Holy Spirit? He is committed to giving us what we should say and do. (v12)
• Whatever anyone else might say or do, we are safe in God's care; there is no need for us to be afraid.

53. 12v13-34 Jesus teaches about trusting and not being afraid

Informing:
- In the crowd are two brothers whose father has died. One of them is keeping to himself everything that their father left, rather than sharing it with his brother as he should have done. Jesus does not tell the brother what to do, but tells a story to encourage each of them (and the others who were listening) to think about what they were doing with their lives.
- Solomon was a king of Israel who had amazing riches which are described in 1 Kings 10, where it says that he was richer than every other king.

Introducing:
- The man in the crowd rightly recognised Jesus as a teacher, one who is concerned about things being put right. However he was trying to use Jesus to get what he wanted. Perhaps his question should have been, "Teacher, my brother won't give me my share of what our father left us. What is the right thing for me to do about that?"
- Having earlier in this chapter spoken about his followers as friends, here Jesus speaks of them as a little flock. In likening them to sheep, he is speaking to them as their shepherd. The words he is saying to them are similar to the words in Psalm 23 where David says that because the Lord is his shepherd, he has everything that he needs.

Inspiring:
- Jesus makes the lovely statement that not only will our Father in heaven give us what we need for daily living, he is also happy to give us his Kingdom. To be given the Kingdom can mean being given:
  1) the provision and protection that come from the King.
  2) the privilege of representing Jesus, having responsibility in the work of the Kingdom.
  3) the power of the Holy Spirit to bring the blessing of Jesus' Kingdom to others - love, joy, peace, healing, and God's message.
  4) a place in heaven.

Instructing:

• Jesus calls us to set our hearts (to focus our lives) on living for him, to trust God for everything we need for ourselves, and to trust God for everything we need to live for his Kingdom.

• It is an adventure of faith in which the more we look to him, the more we will receive from him to show his Kingdom in and through our lives. Although this is very different from the way that others live, it is not meant to scare us. Rather, Jesus shows that it can be a life of peace and freedom from fear.

54. 12v35-48 Jesus teaches about being ready

Informing:
• Wedding feasts such as Jesus talks about in the first story could go on day after day for a week or more. Jesus uses the picture of a man going to a feast like that, with his servants at home not knowing when he will return home.

• In the second story, Jesus describes 4 kinds of servants:

1) The one who fulfils his responsibilities and is rewarded. (v42-44)

2) The one who uses his position selfishly and takes advantage of others. (v45-46)

3) The one who knows what is expected but does not do it. (v47)

4) The one who does not know what is expected of him. (Did someone not tell him, or did he not bother to find out?)(v48)

• These give us a picture of how we are given responsibilities by God for some work in his Kingdom. Jesus is looking for us to discover what is expected of us and to do it, so that we enjoy his reward rather than face his discipline.

Introducing:
• We are like servants in "Jesus' house". There are times when there appears to be no particular work that we are called to do, but Jesus wants us to be ready for action whenever he calls.

• In the first story, Jesus shows that he is a surprising and different sort of master, like one who would look after the needs of his servants by serving them a meal.

• Waiting for Jesus can sometimes be for a short time, like in the wedding feast story, or for a longer time, like in the story of the master going away and leaving his servant in charge.

• Jesus can come to us in our daily lives with something that he wants us to do.

• He can come to us at special times in our lives to involve us in special work for his Kingdom.

• He can come in times of revival when people in an area feel his presence in a special way.

• He will come again finally to the world as he promised.

Inspiring:

• Jesus wants us to be in tune with his Spirit, knowing what he wants and so being what he describes in v37 and v43 as <u>happy</u> servants.

• From Peter's question, it looks as if he is asking whether the disciples are a group with special privileges that Jesus (like the master in the story) would treat in a special way. Jesus answers with another story which shows that if you have a "special" place in Jesus' house, then, rather than having special privileges, you have special responsibilities in making sure that others are provided with what they need. We are to have the same spirit of serving that Jesus has. The greater place of leadership we are given, the more we have a place of giving to others rather than looking to receive from them.

Instructing:

• Be always ready for instant action whenever Jesus calls.

• Be carrying out daily the responsibilities you have been given.

• Be working towards Jesus' coming.

• As Jesus said, if we knew that a thief was coming, we would make sure we were awake to stop him. How much more should we be ready for Jesus who has promised to come to us?

55. 12v49-59 Jesus speaks about facing difficult times

Informing:

• How can Jesus say that he did not come to bring peace? To people he helped (see 7v50; 8v48) he told them to go in peace, and in telling his disciples how to bring God's Kingdom to people, he said that when they came into someone's house, they should offer a greeting of peace (10v5). Jesus did come to bring us peace with God, peace in ourselves, and peace with people who otherwise would not be our friends.

What Jesus is saying here is that when people refuse to accept what he came to bring, then they fight against it, so his coming makes a division between those who accept him and those who do not.

• In v54-59 people are being warned about <u>pride</u> – thinking that they understand God's ways when they did not recognise what was meant by all the wonderful things Jesus was doing. They are being warned too about <u>stubbornness.</u> If they owed someone money, it would be sensible to come to some arrangement with them at the right time rather than leaving it until forced to go to court and have worse to face when they were proved wrong. In a similar way, if they had disagreements with Jesus, he was there at that time to talk with them, and he was giving them the opportunity to have things put right. If they stubbornly refused, they would eventually face God's judgement.

Introducing:

• It is not very often that Jesus talks about his feelings, but here in v49-51 he describes very deep feelings. There are things he still has to do, and he wants to get on with this work so that more and more people can receive all he has for them. It would be like a fire spreading around the world, and to make this happen, he would have to go into, through and out of a time of suffering (like people go into, through and out of the water when they are baptised).

• Jesus not only felt strongly, he also spoke strongly to warn people about having wrong thoughts about him. He says these things, not to condemn them, but to give them the opportunity to have things put right.

Inspiring:

• Fire in the Old Testament indicated God being with his people: 1) showing his glory, 2) speaking to them, 3) purifying them from sin, 4) accepting them (when they brought sacrifices), 5) giving them light.

• Jesus was like a fire doing all these things, but at that time these things were only happening where <u>he</u> was. He was looking forward to the time when he would send the Holy Spirit who would be like a fire in everyone who believes in Jesus, to carry these same things all over the world.

Instructing:

• When we live for Jesus, we should be prepared for some people being against us, even some people who are quite close to us.

• There are times when it is right to warn people strongly about what they are saying and doing, not to show them that they are wrong, but to help them to see what is right.

• We should be trying to understand what God is doing today, so that we are prepared for what is going to happen next.

• If we have to choose to be at peace with Jesus, or to be at peace with someone else, we know which to choose, don't we?

56. 13v1-9 Jesus is looking for people to turn to God

Informing:
  • Pilate (as mentioned in 3v1) was the Roman governor of the region of Judea.
  • Here we have two news stories of that time.
  1) Some Jewish people from the region of Galilee had been killed on Pilate's orders while they were making their animal sacrifices in the temple at Jerusalem.
  2) Some people had been killed in a building accident in Jerusalem.
  All that we know about these incidents is written here, so this is all we need to know about them to get the message that Jesus teaches. From what Jesus says, it is clear that the people thought that if something very bad happens to you, either through the cruelty of others, or the circumstances in your life, then at some time you must have done something really bad. Therefore, they thought, you deserve what has happened.
  • Fig trees were considered to be the most fruitful of all trees. They could produce 3 crops of fruit each year.

Introducing:
  • Having, until this time, shown people much of God's Kingdom through his miracles, healings and teaching, Jesus warns people that they will die/perish/miss out on eternal life if they continue in their old way of living. He shows from the story of the fig tree that he wants to do everything he can to help people to have "fruitful" lives. That means lives that have the good things that come from being in touch with God. • Jesus is like the gardener who wants to give an extra chance to respond.
  • The fig tree in the vineyard is a picture of Israel with its specially privileged place in God's Kingdom. With 3 years of Jesus doing and saying wonderful things, they were as a nation still not receiving him. He is going to do even more to give them the opportunity to respond rightly to him.

Inspiring:
  • There are things here to help us understand our relationship with God:

1) It is not true that people who suffer a lot have done worse things than others.

2) Everyone has failed to live as God wants, and anyone who does not turn to God's ways will miss the life that God gives beyond death.

3) Everyone who does turn to God from their own way of living will not perish; instead they will receive forgiveness, and the Holy Spirit, and new life which will not be lost by death.

4) The time when people have the opportunity to turn to God will not go on for ever.

Instructing:

• We are not to judge people by the bad things that happen to them, or by their experience of suffering.

• We are not to just think and talk about other people's stories, but to make sure that we ourselves are living in a right relationship with God.

• We should not give up too soon on people who look as if they are not responding to God, and with whom there is no sign of anything happening. They may yet come to life if they are given some special love and attention.

57. 13v10-21 Jesus heals a crippled woman

Informing:
• The village or town synagogues had services of worship which included prayers and readings from the Old Testament. Then someone would be asked to give some preaching, after which the men could ask him questions. The women and children sat in a separate section from the men. The leader of the synagogue arranged what happened, so he would have invited Jesus to do the teaching that day.
• The woman's problem in her body was linked to and caused by an evil spirit that had affected her 18 years before. We do not know what she had done or what had happened that had resulted in her being affected in this way. We see here that a person may be affected by an evil spirit not just in their thoughts, words and behaviour, but also in them being unable to live freely because in some way they are "tied up".
• Abraham - see *Informing:* 6. 1v46-56

Introducing:
• From the <u>particular</u> words used in the description we can form a clearer picture of the event:
Jesus is sitting in the raised part of the building and is teaching. Looking around at the people, he sees the woman bent double, twisting her head to look at him. Interrupting his own teaching, he calls out to her, "Woman you are set free from being unwell". He leaves where he is sitting, walks down through the men's section to the section where the woman is, and places his hands on her. She at once straightens up and speaks out, maybe something like, "That's amazing! I have been bent double for 18 years, and now I am healed. Praise God!"
After Jesus rebukes the leader for disapproving, he calls the woman "a daughter of Abraham", showing that she was one of God's chosen people. Others may have had questions about her past, but she is shown acceptance and honour by Jesus.

Inspiring:
• Holy Spirit power was released through Jesus when he spoke the

words and placed his hands on the woman. Holy Spirit power at work shows up any opposing spirit, as there was in the leader. He had invited Jesus to teach and is then angry at what Jesus did. He decides that healing is "work" so should not be done on the Sabbath, and he misses out on what God really wants. With Jesus having done something different from the normal service, and the woman speaking out (which was not usually allowed), the leader realised that they were not under his control. So instead of speaking to them, he speaks to the congregation, hoping to keep them under his control, doing things his way.

• The mustard seed story shows how Holy Spirit power in the Kingdom of God may look very small but it can produce something very big.

• The story of a little yeast in a big batch of dough shows how Holy Spirit power can, without being seen, affect a very large area or group of people.

Instructing:

• Part of serving Jesus is to work with him in untying people from Satan's power.

• We can believe in the Holy Spirit's power to bring answers to long-lasting problems.

• We should recognise times when it is right for us to do something different from what is expected, like when Jesus took healing to the woman during the service.

• We should put ourselves (as the woman did) in the place where Jesus can see us, speak to us, and bring his touch to our lives.

• We should guide people away from the danger of giving room to evil spirits as it can lead to long-lasting problems in their lives.

58. 13v22-30 Jesus speaks about who will be saved

Informing:

• From the way that Jesus answered the question, "being saved" means having a place in God's Kingdom, a happy place of acceptance, safety, security and peace, a place in heaven free from anything that would harm us. That place is like "God's house", a place to live for those who have chosen to trust their lives to him.

• Abraham, Isaac and Jacob were the people from whom the Jews were descended.

Introducing:

• Jesus shows concern for these Jewish people who are spending time with him. They would have thought that because they were Jews, they were already in God's Kingdom. Jesus tells them that each person must individually choose to come into God's Kingdom. The way in was open for them at that time, and they should come in without delay. He tells them to strive, to try hard to get in, not because the door is difficult to get through, but because there are things that could get in their way. (Things in ourselves, some other people and the Devil try to stop us from going God's way.) If they put off deciding, that meant they were continuing to live for what is not right, and so were opposing God's Kingdom. There would come a time when the opportunity to enter God's Kingdom would come to an end, and if they had not gone in, they would bitterly regret missing out on the blessing which had been there for them to choose. The only way for them to have a place in God's Kingdom is to have their own personal friendship with him.

• Some people that they thought were sure to be in God's Kingdom would be among the last to choose to go in, while others would be there that they would not have expected.

Inspiring:

• The Holy Spirit brings Jesus to us in different ways. For example, we might feel him near in a church service or time of worship (this is like "we ate and drank with you"), and when we hear or read the Bible (this is like "you taught in our streets"). These experiences are good, but the Holy Spirit, along with wanting Jesus to come to us, wants us to come to Jesus, to go through the door of trusting our lives to him.

• The Holy Spirit brings us into a worldwide family, people from east, west, north and south who love Jesus, and in heaven we will share with all the others who through the ages have lived for God.

Instructing:

• We have here a good outline for sharing with others how to be "saved", that is to come into God's Kingdom, live for him and enjoy heaven after we die.

1) There is a particular door to go in, a door of forgiveness which we go through when we leave our own way and accept God's way.

2) The door into God's Kingdom is open because Jesus died for us.

3) Anyone can enter if they accept God's way.

4) There is a limit on the time that the door is open.

5) Putting off deciding to go in is deciding to be against God.

6) There will be great joy for all who go in, and great regret for those who do not.

59. 13v31-35 Jesus goes towards Jerusalem

Informing:

• Herod, who governed the regions of Galilee and Perea, was the one who had put John the Baptist in prison (3v19-20) and had then had him killed (9v7-9).

• Jesus was at this point in an area which Herod governed.

• Jerusalem was the centre of the life of God's people, where they came together to pray, to offer sacrifices, to celebrate festivals and so enjoy friendship with God. The leaders were based there, so at the times when the Jews turned away from God, it had been the place where the decisions had been made to kill the prophets who were speaking God's message to the people.

Introducing:

• Jesus shows his strong commitment to his work and to his people. He is going to keep doing his work and not be stopped either by the threats of enemies like Herod, or by the advice of others like these Pharisees. Also it is too late to stop him as in a short time he will have completed all he set out to do.

• In saying about prophets being killed in Jerusalem, Jesus is pointing out the strange fact that the place where prophets should be most welcomed had been the place where they had been most rejected. Jesus knew that the main opposition would come to him, not from an enemy of God's people like Herod, but from leaders at the centre of God's people. Knowing this, he was moving on, not to avoid death but to go towards it.

• Jesus spoke of Jerusalem as being like a parent with children, because the leaders (like parents) of God's people were based there. His deep feeling of sadness is shown in what he says. His tender love is shown in his likening himself to a mother hen protecting her chicks. His saying, "How often" shows that he has an ongoing love which has not stopped even though he has been rejected.

Inspiring:

• Some people think that everything that happens in the world happens because God wants it to happen. From what Jesus says here, it is clear that this is not true. He says that what he had continually wanted to happen had not happened because people had chosen to say no to him. The Holy Spirit brings God's love to people but they can choose to accept or reject that love. However, God is able to work everything that happens into fulfilling his ultimate purpose; so even Jerusalem's rejection of Jesus would be used to fulfil God's plan.

• When people want to welcome God into their lives, they will see that Jesus is from God and accept him gladly. Whenever people reject Jesus, they are shutting the door on God being with them, and so it is like their home being left empty.

Instructing:

• We should not think that everyone in a particular group of people will think the same. Some Pharisees wanted to kill Jesus. These Pharisees warned him of danger.

• We should not let enemies or friends stop us from completing what God has given us to do.

• When people do not receive what we want to give them from God, we should not stop loving them. We should keep on wanting the best for them.

60. 14v1-24 A Pharisee invites Jesus to a meal

Informing:
 • The Sabbath Day was given by God to be a gift of rest, a time for people to worship together and as a sign of God's commitment to provide for his people. They would have enough for their needs from working six days each week. The Pharisees and Teachers of the Law had turned the Sabbath into a set of rules to obey.
 • The question about the Sabbath and healing kept being asked (6v6-11, 13v10-17). Jesus once again teaches that in the Sabbath being given for rest, it is not there to stop people doing good.
 • The man suffered from dropsy, a condition where there is swelling because of too much fluid in the body. It could have a number of causes.
 • Jesus mentions the resurrection of people who are righteous, that is the coming to life again of those who have lived trusting God, the time which he again (as in 13v29) describes as a heavenly feast.

Introducing:
 • Jesus noticed the sick man. It is as Jesus was going into the house that the man was there in front of him; the man was not an invited guest. Jesus took hold of him (showing his acceptance), healed him and "let him go". The phrase used is the same as in 13v12, so it speaks of being released, being given freedom.
 • Jesus noticed the way that some people were watching him, trying to catch him out. It says in verse 3 that Jesus <u>answered</u> them (not "asked" as in some Bibles). They had not used words but were questioning him by the way they looked at him. He knew what was in their minds.
 • He noticed the guests trying to get the "best" places at the table, looking to be seen as important. Even though he was a guest too, Jesus challenged them about what they were doing, and taught them about being humble.
 • He noticed that the Pharisee was giving the meal not to bless people but to get the appreciation of the guests. He challenged him to be doing things that would bless others without getting anything back.
 • He noticed the man who rightly said about the happiness of those at

the Kingdom of God feast in heaven. He challenged him to make sure that he himself did not miss out, and to be someone who helped others to come to the feast.

Inspiring:
• The Holy Spirit brings a free invitation to the Kingdom of God. God has done everything that is needed for us. All we have to do is to accept his invitation. People miss out by making other things more important: possessions (field), or work (oxen for ploughing), or family (just married). The Kingdom of God does not replace any of these things, but puts them in the proper place in our lives.

• The story of the feast, as well as being about heaven, is also a picture of revival when God "prepares a feast" to be enjoyed. At such times there are those who would be expected to participate who do not because of their pride, putting their own things first. There are others, who would never have thought themselves likely to be accepted by God, who will enjoy what has been prepared. Some of them, because they feel so unworthy have to be "made" to come, not against their will, but to overcome their thought that such good things could not possibly be for them.

Instructing:
• Let us not be so taken up with what we are doing that we miss the person in need right in front of us.

• Let us allow God to place us where he wants us to be.

• Let us work to be a blessing to others, to be a giver.

• Let us not allow <u>anything</u> to get in the way of us enjoying what God has given us.

• As Jesus' servants, let us be ready to invite others to the feast.

61. 14v25-35 Jesus speaks about following him

Informing:

• In verse 26 Jesus uses the word "hate" in a way that is different from the way we use it. We know that Jesus expects us to <u>love</u> our families. In 1 John 2v9 we read that anyone who says he is in the light but hates his brother is still in darkness. Here (v26), Jesus uses the idea of hating someone to mean <u>not choosing them</u>.

• So becoming a true follower of Jesus means deciding that we will always choose:

1) what Jesus wants rather than what anyone else wants.

2) what Jesus wants rather than what we ourselves want. This is "carrying our cross", deciding that what we want can "die" so that what Jesus wants can happen in and through us.

3) what Jesus wants rather than anything else, so we are willing to set aside anything we have or could have that does not fit in with us doing what Jesus wants.

Introducing:

• Many people travelled with Jesus who did not give their lives to him. Here Jesus calls the people to make a clear decision to follow him, to think carefully about what this would mean for them and then to give their lives wholeheartedly to following him. He warns them about beginning to follow but not continuing. This would result in:

1) them being made fun of (like the man failing to complete the tower).

2) them being ruled by Satan (like the king not prepared for fighting the enemy then having to accept his demands).

3) them failing to be and do what God wanted (they were meant to be like salt, making a difference wherever they were).

Inspiring:

• In teaching about being a disciple of Jesus, this passage speaks about having the power to be kept from turning away from following Jesus, having the strength to build, having the power to fight, and having the ability to make a difference. The Holy Spirit is the one who gives us power, strength and ability for these things in Jesus' Kingdom. Faced with the challenge, "Do you have the power to always choose what Jesus wants, whatever others say, whatever you think, and whatever you may have to give up or go without?" the only honest answer we can give is, "No, even if I want to, I am not strong enough on my own to do that." That is the place that Jesus wants us to come to, so that we will fully rely on the Holy Spirit's power working in us to keep us close to Jesus every day.

Instructing:

• If we are prepared to commit ourselves fully to Jesus, the Holy Spirit is prepared to commit himself fully to us, so that we need not fear that we might begin well but then not be able to continue all our lives as Christians.

• If we make that clear decision now, it will help to keep us making the right choices when new situations and challenges come our way throughout our lives. Jesus told us these things so that we will not fail.

62. 15v1-10 Jesus explains why he is with "sinners"

Informing:
- Tax collectors – see *Informing: 22. 5v27-32*
- The word "sinners" is used here to describe people who were not religious, who were not part of the community that worshipped God.
- Jesus has just said that those who have ears to hear should hear (14v35), and here is a large group who accept his open invitation; they want to hear him.
- There is a special happiness in finding something that we have lost, which leads us to tell friends and share with them our feelings about it.
- Angels – see *Informing: 3. 1v11-25*

Introducing:
- In accepting these people, Jesus is not saying their way of life is right, but rather that he is happy to help them to be different.
- To show his feelings about these people, Jesus gives a picture of himself as the good shepherd in the story. He is very happy to have found them. (A bad shepherd, like some of the Pharisees and Teachers of the Law, would not have been bothered about one sheep lost from a hundred.)
- Jesus is happy, the "tax collectors and sinners" are happy, and Jesus is calling on the Pharisees and Teachers of the Law to be happy with him at these people coming to learn God's ways.
- Jesus is not satisfied with the number of people who have already been put right with God. He gives special attention and care to the work of bringing others back to God. He loves them and thinks of them as belonging to him.

Inspiring:
- What was happening here is what could be called a "revival", a time when the Holy Spirit was drawing a whole large group of people to Jesus. The Holy Spirit works to bring back to God people who have gone away from him. What Jesus was doing at this time, the Holy Spirit is still doing.
- There is a spirit of happiness in the work of Jesus' Kingdom. In Romans

14v17 his Kingdom is described as having righteousness, peace and joy in the Holy Spirit.

• Heaven celebrates every new person who finds a place of belonging in Jesus. There has been rejoicing in heaven about you!

Instructing:

• This passage gives us a challenge to be like Jesus. We should be so welcoming to ordinary non-church people that they will want to come and hear what we have to say.

• While we should give attention to our life with others who love and follow Jesus, we should also be giving time and attention to helping in some way to bring in those who are outside so that they can find a place of knowing Jesus and being "at home" with God.

63. 15v11-32 Jesus tells a story about a father's love

Informing:
• In this special story, Jesus explains more fully to the Pharisees and Teachers of the Law (who are like the older son), why he is welcoming people who are like the younger son.
• The younger son asked for his inheritance, which would normally have been given to him after his father's death. When an inheritance was divided, the eldest son was given a double amount. This would cover the expenses of having overall responsibility for the family. So a third would have been given to the younger son and two thirds to the older son. So when the younger son came back, it did not mean that the older son would lose anything of his personal third.
• For a Jew to join with someone from another country was considered unlawful. (Acts 10v28)
• As part of showing that the Jews were different from other nations, there were some animals that they were not allowed to eat. Pigs were among these animals that were called "unclean".

Introducing:
• Jesus, in welcoming the tax collectors and "sinners" is likening himself to the father in the story, who is a picture of our heavenly Father showing his love for us.
The father goes out to the son who had been away. He is in a hurry to welcome him home. He accepts him, even before the son says anything. He straight away gives him everything that shows he is properly and fully back in his place in the family.
He goes out to the older son who does not want to come in to the celebration.
Even when that son speaks in an angry dishonouring way, the father says to him the beautiful words, "My boy, you are always with me, and everything I have is yours."
• Jesus is making it clear that his love for the tax collectors and "sinners" does not make his love for the Pharisees and Teachers of the Law any less.

He wants them all to be happy and to be at home with him and with one another.

Inspiring:

• What happened to the young man in the far away country is what the Holy Spirit does for people who have gone away from God. The Holy Spirit can help them to <u>remember</u> Father's love for them, to <u>realise</u> where they have gone wrong, and to <u>return</u> to their proper relationship with Father.

Instructing:

• Lessons from the younger son: 1) However attractive it may seem, going our own way rather than God's way will always result in loss, never in gain. 2) Whatever mess we have made in our lives, we can be brought back to a proper place in God's family because he still loves us.

• Lessons from the older son: 1) We should be careful that in trying to live a life that pleases God, we do not just do things <u>for</u> him while we miss having the same heart as he has. 2) If we are close to Father, we should welcome and celebrate with people who come to God after being far away from his ways.

• The story that Jesus told is unfinished, and so makes us think what we would do. Did the older son accept what the father said and then go into the party? Would you? There will be times when we are angry or have a wrong attitude which the Holy Spirit will challenge us about. He wants to bring us into the full enjoyment that Father has for us. Let us not miss out by thinking wrongly about others or about Father's love for us.

64. 16v1-18 Jesus teaches about money

Informing:

• We saw in chapter 15 that at this time, Jesus' followers included tax collectors. They were well known for their wrong use of money, charging as much as they could to make themselves rich. Now Jesus teaches them and his other followers to be generous to others. This will result in them having more friends, and, by living for God's Kingdom, they will have an eternal home in heaven.

• While tax collectors had served riches instead of serving God, Pharisees thought that they could serve God while at the same time making themselves rich.

• Pharisees claimed to follow the teachings of the Old Testament laws and prophets, but they invented ways of avoiding some laws. Jesus refers to their making easy ways for a man to divorce his wife and then remarry for reasons that were not in line with what God had said.

• The Pharisees did not like the way that since John the Baptist and Jesus started preaching, people without a religious background were being accepted as serving God. They felt that such people were like uninvited "gatecrashers" coming in and spoiling their party! Jesus explains that this is not an ignoring of the Law and the Prophets, but rather that in following Jesus, these people will more fully obey these teachings than those who followed the Pharisees' faulty rules.

• In the story, the manager changes the amount that people owed to his boss to less than it was. That made them happy with him, so that when he lost his job, they would be friendly to him. His boss, though unhappy at losing out, was impressed at the manager's cleverness.

Introducing:

• In telling the story, Jesus is not suggesting that what the manager did was right and good. Rather he is showing how clever people can be in using money for their own purposes. He is challenging his followers to be just as thoughtful (in a right way) in how they can use money for the purposes of the Kingdom of heaven.

Inspiring:

• The Holy Spirit sometimes uses stories to help us understand and think through God's message to us, and sometimes he uses direct words like when we are told clearly that we cannot serve God and also serve riches. The same words, which encourage and bless those who want God's ways, challenge and offend those who do not. Our response to the Holy Spirit's words shows what is going on in our hearts.

Instructing:

• Money is not meant to govern how we live but is to be used creatively and thoughtfully for Jesus' Kingdom. God is looking to see how we can use what we have been given. When we can be trusted to do the right thing with ordinary things like money, God will trust us with special responsibilities in the work of his Kingdom.

65. 16v19-31 Jesus tells a story about a rich man and a poor man

Informing:

• Jesus teaches a powerful lesson using ideas that the Pharisees were familiar with. They thought of heaven as sitting with Abraham, and they expected to be there. Jesus had already warned (13v28) that some who thought like that would not be there.

• The reason for this story is in 16v14 where the Pharisees had sneered at Jesus for teaching that wanting riches for yourself did not fit with serving God.

• The rich man lived in luxury every day so he had plenty with which he could have cared for the beggar. He had no excuse, as he had seen the beggar whenever he went in and out of his house. He knew him by name as he later asks Abraham to send Lazarus.

• The rich man was a Jew, he called Abraham, "father", and Abraham called him, "son/child" but that did not guarantee him a place in heaven.

• The reason why the beggar had suffered evil things in his life was because the rich man had not used properly the good things that he had been blessed with.

• The rich man having five brothers was used by Jesus as a picture to show that among the Pharisees it was not just one or two who were living wrongly, but the whole "family" of them.

Introducing:

• Jesus told this story because he cared enough about the Pharisees and others to warn them about the way they were living before it would be too late. He is giving them the opportunity to change and to realise what will happen to them if they do not.

• A special thing about the story is that the beggar's name was Lazarus which is the same name as the man that Jesus did later bring back to life (see John 11). It says (John 11v45) that as a result, many Jews believed in him, but some went to the Pharisees who began to plan to kill him. So as Jesus pointed out in the story, if they did not listen to Moses and the

Prophets, they would not be convinced even if someone were to rise from death.

Inspiring:

• "Moses and the Prophets" is a way of speaking about the books of the Old Testament. The Holy Spirit speaks through Moses and the Prophets and the other parts of the Bible. We find in the Bible all we need to know about how to be right with God, how to live as he wants us to live and be welcomed into heaven when we die.

Instructing:

• We can learn from Jesus' example that there is a right time and a right way to warn people strongly about their way of living, using words and ideas that they will understand. We should do it from love because we want them to come into the blessing of living God's way.

• There is the challenge to us in what Jesus says to make sure that our way of living is right. It is not good enough just to say, "I'm a Christian." We have responsibility to use the good things that God has given us to bless others.

• The big lesson in the story is that if people do not decide to change to God's ways in this life, it will be too late for them to do so after death.

66. 17v1-10 Jesus teaches forgiveness

Informing:
• The word (in v1,2) that in some Bibles is translated "causes to sin" means more than that. The word that Jesus used means something that traps or trips people up, something that gets in their way. In chapter 16, the rich man got in the way of the beggar having enough to eat, making him suffer needlessly. The Pharisees got in the way of people finding the right way by teaching things that were different from what God wanted.
• A millstone was a big circular stone that was used to grind corn.

Introducing:
• Jesus shows here his care for "little ones" (children and any others who might be easily led into something which harms them and takes them away from God's ways). Jesus saying, "<u>these</u> little ones" shows that there were children there with Jesus when he was teaching.
• The disciples ask Jesus to do something which will give them more faith for them to be able to forgive. They are saying either, "It's hard to believe that we have to do that", or "It's hard to believe that we would be able to do that. We need your help".
• Jesus' story about how people treat their servants is not saying what he is like, or what the right thing to do is, but rather what it would be common to do. Jesus is explaining, "You don't think there is anything particularly special about a servant doing his job, so why you should you think there is anything particularly special about forgiving people if you are serving God?" It's normal, so forgiving is not a matter of having faith to do it; it is a matter of doing what we are told to do.
• Jesus' comments about faith are not suggesting that we should go about showing that we trust him by moving trees into the sea! He is teaching that being in touch with him, trusting him, means that we will have all the power that we need to do what God wants, whatever that is.

Inspiring:
• While forgiving is normal to Jesus, it can only become normal to us if we are serving Jesus as he wants by having the Holy Spirit to help us and

change us. The Holy Spirit's help will keep us from doing things that would hinder other people. The Holy Spirit's help will teach us how to speak when someone has done wrong, in a way that is not to punish them but to help them to put things right. The Holy Spirit's help will make forgiveness more of a normal way of life for us.

• When Jesus says in verse 3, "forgive him" it is a command, but in verse 4, although some Bibles don't show it, Jesus says, "you will forgive him". He is not saying here that you <u>have</u> to forgive again and again, but rather, if you begin to forgive, you will find that it becomes the way that you live.

Instructing:

• We are to watch ourselves so that we do not become a hindrance to others by discouraging them, diverting them (making them turn away), or detaining them (holding them back from going on).

• When a brother (that's a name used for Christians) does something wrong against us, we could be trapped or tripped up by the hurt it causes us; we could be trapped or tripped up by becoming bitter if we are not willing to forgive. It is important to do something about it because our friendship is broken, and if we explain what he has done and why it is important to us, it makes a way for him to be helped to put things right. If we ignore it, he may do the same to others and become a hindrance for them. We do not want to be living in unforgiveness, as it is one of the biggest hindrances that we can allow in our lives.

67. 17v11-19 Ten men are healed of leprosy

Informing:
- Leprosy - see *Informing:* 20. 5v12-16
- Samaria - see *Informing:* 43. 9v46- 62
- All ten were healed of leprosy by Jesus' power, but for nine of them that is all they received. To the one who came back, Jesus words were that his faith had <u>saved</u> him. That means, because he trusted Jesus, he was brought into a place of wholeness, safety and protection.

Introducing:
- Jesus heals people in many different ways. In chapter 5 he touched the man with leprosy; here he gives the ten an instruction to obey without saying what will happen.
- They shout to ask for mercy, which is to ask for his help in their suffering, and he brings healing to them without asking them to do anything for him in return.
- He healed them all even though nine did not care enough to come back to him. We would have expected that they would have wanted to be with him and to get to know him better.

Inspiring:
- The Holy Spirit had been at work in the lives of these men. They recognised Jesus (they called his name), and they used a word for him that the disciples used, "Master" meaning someone with authority. They believed that he would do something to help them. How did they know that? They must have heard from others about Jesus and what he was doing, like in healing other people who had leprosy (5v12-15; 7v22).
- The Holy Spirit can use <u>our</u> experiences of Jesus to point others to him and to give them hope that he may do something to help them.

Instructing:
- In times of suffering we can call on Jesus for help.
- Jesus may sometimes ask us to take a step of obedience as a way of then receiving what he has for us.

• We are sometimes loud in shouting when we need Jesus' help. Like the Samaritan, we should be loud in praising and thanking Jesus for what he has done for us.

• We should not think that everyone in a group is the same. There could be one, an unexpected one, who is the most open to Jesus.

68. 17v 20-37 Pharisees ask when God's Kingdom will come

Informing:
• The Pharisees (and the disciples) probably thought of the Kingdom of God as the nation of Israel coming into a place of power in the world with God's presence and blessing on them in a special way. Jesus gives a different picture.

• What Jesus said to the Pharisees can mean either that the Kingdom of God is <u>among</u> you or the Kingdom of God is <u>in</u> you. In asking about when it would come, they did not recognise that the King, Jesus was right there <u>among</u> them! They were looking for the Kingdom to come to their land, and missed allowing God to be King <u>in</u> their lives.

• While in one sense the Kingdom of God has already come in Jesus, Jesus speaks to the disciples of the sudden coming of God's Kingdom <u>completely</u> at a special time in the future.

• The stories of Noah (Genesis 6) and Lot (Genesis 19) were both of a righteous man living among evil people who would not change their ways. Then God's judgement suddenly came; the righteous man was saved and the evil destroyed.

• God's judgement will come to wherever in the world his ways are being opposed, like vultures (birds of prey) go to wherever there is a dead body in the countryside.

Introducing:
• The Pharisees were thinking, "The Kingdom of God is not here yet", and Jesus was saying that it was already there. The disciples would have been thinking, "The Kingdom of God is here now!" so Jesus tells them that not everything of the Kingdom was going to happen there and then. He speaks of:

1) the days of the Son of Man, that is the time when he was there with them.

2) then a time of him suffering and being rejected.

3) some times after that when there would not be the obvious signs of the Kingdom that were there when Jesus was with them.

4) a time when he would suddenly appear to the whole world, bringing

the full blessings of the Kingdom to those who are right with God, and judgement on all those who oppose God's ways.

• Son of Man - see *Introducing:* 21. 5v17-26. Jesus had already used the name "Son of Man" in speaking of his suffering (9v22) and his sudden coming (12v40).

Inspiring:

• God's Kingdom is in us and among us by the presence of the Holy Spirit.

• The Holy Spirit will help us to see when God's Kingdom is right beside us.

• The Holy Spirit will keep us in God's Kingdom way of living (like Noah and Lot were kept) when people all around us are living in a different way.

• The Holy Spirit will keep us ready to be taken to be with Jesus (when he comes again or when we die).

Instructing:

• Although Jesus is teaching about the day when he will come again to the world, the lessons apply to other times too.

• We should not put off being in a right relationship with God.

• We can be a sign of God's Kingdom to others (like Noah and Lot were) by living in the way that Jesus wants us to.

• Especially in times when it seems that nothing much is happening, we should beware of going away from the road that God has given us, to follow people who claim to have something special.

• The call of God's Kingdom should be more important to us that anything else from our past. We should live daily in touch with Jesus, ready to respond quickly to him.

69. 18v1-14 Jesus says to keep on praying

Informing:

• The woman whose husband had died was being bothered by someone, who was perhaps claiming that something that belonged to her was his, like, for instance, a piece of land. She goes to the judge as he is the person in the community who has the authority to decide matters of the law. She hopes that he will deal with the matter and stop the person bothering her.

• The two stories fit together. It is as if someone listening to the first one is thinking, "Well, I pray all the time so I'm ok." then Jesus tells the second story about a Pharisee like them!

• When the tax collector asked for "mercy" as the sinner, he uses a different word from the word used by the lepers in chapter 17. There they asked for help in their suffering. Here the word used means "I have done wrong; please do something to make things right between us."

• Jesus says that the tax-collector was justified, that means put right and accepted by God.

Introducing:

• Jesus is not saying that God is like the judge so that if we keep on praying for long enough God will eventually answer us. Rather he is saying that if someone like the judge might give an answer to someone he doesn't care about, how much more we can be sure that God, who has chosen us to be his own, will surely do the right thing for us at the right time. Sometimes there may be a delay, when we are calling day and night to him, but when he answers he makes things happen quickly. He will not neglect us.

• Continuing to pray is not to remind God or to persuade him, but to keep expressing our trust in him.

• We can trust that sooner or later Jesus puts things right for his people. The test of our trust in him is whether we keep on believing during the times when we see no sign of it happening.

• Jesus likes humble people. He does not like it when people look down on others.

Inspiring:

• All the words that are used in the Bible are there because the Holy Spirit wants to say something special through those particular words. In places where it is not exactly clear what the words mean, it is often because we can learn from the different possible ways we can understand what is written. In verse 7 after talking about God answering the call of his people it says that he is <u>longsuffering</u> over them. Different translations of the Bible use different words to try to express some of the meaning of these words. Here are some of the ideas that could be found in the words:

• God does not mind us keeping on bringing our needs to him for him to do something about it.

• There is sometimes a waiting time before God answers us, but his answer will then come quickly.

• When God's people are suffering, and things at that time are not being put right for them, God suffers with them and feels their pain.

• The way that the word "longsuffering" is used elsewhere in the Bible is about God waiting and holding back for a time before judging people who are in the wrong. This is to give them time in which they might change from their wrongdoing and so escape his judgement. So when we are wronged by other people and we want God to put things right for us, sometimes his delay in answering us is to give those people who have wronged us the opportunity to change.

Instructing:

• Keep praying. Keep trusting. Keep humble.

• We can be tempted to stop praying when God does not seem to be answering our prayer, or when we have done something wrong and we feel ashamed about it. Jesus makes it clear that God wants us to keep talking to him about our needs, and not to stay away from him when we have done wrong, but rather to humbly trust him to accept us and change us.

70. 18v15-27 Jesus speaks about entering his Kingdom

Informing:

• People brought children for Jesus to touch them because they recognised that he could in some way bless them (like when Simeon spoke about baby Jesus in the temple in 2v28).

• We are not told what particular kind of leader the man was, but he would have been someone who made decisions for other people. Here he is looking for Jesus' decision for him.

• When talking about the same thing, the man speaks about <u>receiving eternal life,</u>

Jesus speaks of <u>receiving and entering the Kingdom of God</u>, while those who heard him speak about <u>being saved</u>.

• The hearers' surprise at Jesus' words could have come from a commonly held idea that people who were rich were so because God had blessed them, and that he had blessed them because he approved of them.

• Jesus questions why the man calls him, "Good Teacher". If the man is saying that Jesus is like God, then he ought to be ready to do whatever Jesus says, but we see later that he is not.

Introducing:

• Jesus shows that he welcomes children and considers them to be special to him, and he is displeased when anyone gets in their way.

• A kingdom belongs to the king and whoever he chooses to share that kingdom with. Jesus has already told his disciples that they share in God's Kingdom (12v32) and he says here that children have a part in it too.

• Jesus invites children to come to him, not just to learn about him but to know him as a friend. In the same way, Jesus invited the man to come with him. What a wonderful invitation this was! The man was being invited to join the disciples, to become one of the group going with Jesus. How sad it is that he did not appreciate it.

• Jesus' Kingdom is something that is received, accepted. That means:

1) It is something very simple, like the children coming to Jesus and allowing him to be their friend.

2) It is impossible for anyone to do anything by themselves to get into Jesus' Kingdom. It is something which is given by God through what Jesus has done.

3) Jesus does not force his Kingdom on anyone; it is offered, and a person can either receive it or reject it.

Inspiring:

• What the disciples did to the people bringing children shows that it is possible to be following Jesus, to be working for him, and to still have some old ways of thinking which are far from the Holy Spirit's ways, and so need correcting. As we face new situations, the Holy Spirit will show us where we need to change our thinking.

• The man who spoke to Jesus looked impressive. He called Jesus, "Good Teacher", he said he had tried to follow God's ways since he was a boy, he was asking about eternal life. However, he was not at all in tune with the Holy Spirit because he was not willing to give his life to Jesus. He wanted eternal life, but not if it meant him giving up his own way of life. He probably never knew how powerful money was in his life until then. Perhaps too he wanted to stay as a leader rather than become a follower.

Instructing:

• Be glad that however young you are, Jesus Kingdom is for you. Children don't have to become like adults to come into Jesus' Kingdom, adults have to become like children.

• Let us beware of making the mistake that the disciples did when they told people that what they were doing was wrong, when Jesus thought otherwise. We should be careful not to get in the way of anyone who is coming to Jesus or trying to bring others to him.

71. 18v28-34 Jesus speaks about suffering for his Kingdom

Informing:
- There are different kinds of "leaving" for the sake of the Kingdom of God.
- Leaving to enter the Kingdom, like when the rich man was called to leave behind his riches.
- Leaving to follow the call of the Kingdom, like Peter when he left his work to go with Jesus (5v11).
- Leaving for a short while, like Peter (who was married) leaving his wife and home (4v38) to travel with Jesus. In later years, his wife travelled with him. (1 Corinthians 9v5.)
- Leaving for a long time, like people following God's call to live in another part of the world.
- Leaving that happens when family members react against someone living for Jesus and then want nothing more to do with them.
- Leaving that happens when a Christian is badly treated and is put in prison, or is no longer able to be with his family.
- Leaving family life, like when someone is called by God to stay single in order to serve God in a special way.
- Jesus spoke about doing what the Old Testament prophets had written about him. The disciples did not know what he was talking about. They did not have Bibles of their own to read like we have. One of the passages describing what the Messiah would suffer is Isaiah 53.
- Jesus spoke about being handed over to "Gentiles". This word means "nations" and is used to describe people who are not Jews, so in this case it refers to the Romans who ruled at that time in Israel.

Introducing:
- Jesus' suffering and death was all part of God's plan. It was described hundreds of years before by the Old Testament prophets (although they would not have known the full meaning of all that they were given to say). Jesus knew the plan and willingly gave himself to fulfilling it. So, after Peter had said about what <u>he</u> had given up to obey the call of God's Kingdom, Jesus describes what it is going to cost <u>him</u> to obey God's call in

his life.

• Jesus guarantees that no one who lives for his Kingdom is going to be disappointed in the end. They are going to get back much more than they have ever had to go without. Even when at times it costs us something to go his way, Jesus says that he will more than pay us back either in this life or when we are in heaven. Also when we give our lives to Jesus, we become part of his world-wide family with all other Christians as our brothers and sisters.

• Jesus told his disciples things he knew they would not understand at the time, so that later, when the things happened, they would see that it had all been part of his plan.

Inspiring:

• One of the things which shows that the Bible is inspired (breathed into) by the Holy Spirit, is the way in which some things were written about hundreds of years before they happened, like details about the suffering and death of Jesus.

• Sometimes the Holy Spirit may be saying things to us which we do not understand because we have not yet got to know the part of the Bible that explains it. Knowing the Bible will help us to understand what the Holy Spirit is saying and doing now.

• When the Holy Spirit gives us pictures or words that we do not understand immediately, it is good to make a note of them, as they may be special for us at a later time when something happens and we then remember what the Holy Spirit has already shown us.

Instructing:

• When we have to leave behind or go without things in order to follow Jesus, it is good to remind ourselves that amongst the "much more" that we will have is Jesus' presence, power, peace and purpose to fill our lives.

• If there are times when we have to be apart from our family to serve Jesus, it does not mean that we should stop caring for them and loving them. Jesus calls us to honour our parents, and to love and care for our families, even if, and maybe especially if they do not understand why we have to be where Jesus has called us to be.

72. 18v35-43 Jesus gives sight to a blind man

Informing:

• In the Old Testament, Jericho was the first town to be taken by the Israelites in the land which God promised them. God's power was seen at that time by the walls falling down (Joshua 6). Here God's power is seen there again, this time in Jesus.

• The crowds spoke of Jesus as "Jesus of Nazareth". This is what he was commonly known as.

• All through Luke's book, crowds appear wherever Jesus is, to hear him and to be healed. The crowd with Jesus as he was going into the town would have been people going, as he was, to Jerusalem for the Passover Festival season.

• The words used about the man getting his sight is the word "see again" which shows that the man had been able to see at one time in his life and then had gone blind, and had to beg as his only way of getting what he needed to live.

Introducing:

• The blind man calls out to Jesus as "Son of David" which is a title which was given to the Messiah. Jesus himself speaks about this later (20v41). The Son of David would be a king like David in the Old Testament and a king whose kingdom would last for ever. The blind man must have heard about what Jesus had been saying and doing in other places, and decided that he was God's specially chosen king. When he speaks to Jesus he calls him, "Lord".

• Jesus stops for this one man. He was at some distance from him as Jesus did not hear him when he first called for help. There is a reason why Jesus commanded that the man be brought to him. Jesus was surrounded by a crowd of people. In Luke 12v1 the crowd was so big that people were trampling on one another. If Jesus had just gone to where the man's call was coming from, there was the danger that the crowd would move in front of him in that direction, and may have trampled on the blind man who was sitting on the ground. When Jesus called out a command for the man to be brought, everyone knew what was happening and so could make way for him.

• Jesus' wonderful question asked the man what he wanted Jesus to do for him. The man said "that I may see again", and Jesus simply said, "See again!" and it happened.

As soon as it happened it says that the man followed Jesus. This shows that Jesus was immediately on the move again.

Inspiring:

• Once again we read of people, whom we would have expected to be in tune with the Holy Spirit, who show by what they say that they are not. In chapter 18 the Pharisee did not realise the tax collector's place of importance to God, the disciples did not realise the children's place of importance to God, and here some people in the crowd did not realise the blind beggar's place of importance to God.

• Jesus said to the man that his faith had saved him. When, like him, we recognise Jesus as God's specially chosen one and we open our lives to him, the Holy Spirit can come into our lives and do whatever is needed to bring God's blessings to us.

Instructing:

• There are people who will at times try to get in the way of us being close to Jesus. We should not let them stop us. We are important to Jesus.

• We should take care not to be so caught up in being in the "Jesus crowd" that we miss people on the edges who are in need of being brought to Jesus for his help.

• There are times when it is as if Jesus is passing by, times when his power is available for something special to happen in our lives. We should make use of those opportunities while we can, or we may find that the opportunity is gone, and Jesus has moved on.

• We should take the opportunities God gives us to be a "link in the chain" for people in their experience of Jesus. At some time before, someone must have talked with the blind beggar about Jesus, and that was how the blind man knew what Jesus could do for him. The person who had spoken to the blind man perhaps wished that he could have done something more for him, but he did what he could at the time, and Jesus did the rest later!

73. 19v1-10 Zacchaeus meets Jesus

Informing:
   • Jericho was a rich city. Springs in the surrounding land made it good for growing trees, plants and flowers. As a military and business centre, where roads used by traders crossed one another, it was a centre for collecting taxes and customs.
   • Zacchaeus, as the chief tax collector, would have had to give an agreed amount to the Roman government, and then been able to keep however much more than that he could get people to pay. (Tax collectors - see *Informing:* 22. 5v27-32)
   • The sycamore tree mentioned was different from the type usually known by that name. It was a common fruit tree which grew figs on it. It makes no difference to us what type of tree Zacchaeus climbed, but it shows that whoever told the writer, Luke about it must have been there at the time, and noticed.
   • The idea of paying back four times as much came from laws in the Old Testament. If a sheep was stolen (Exodus 22v1), the thief had to pay back four.
   • "Sons of Abraham" was used to describe people who were accepted by God as part of his chosen people. John the Baptist had made it clear (3v8) that this meant living God's way, not just being born a Jew.
   • Zacchaeus did not say that he would stop being a tax collector, and he did not have to. John the Baptist (3v12,13) said that what tax collectors should do to show that they had turned to God's way was to be fair and to not collect more money than they should.

Introducing:
   • Jesus went from the poor blind beggar to a rich tax collector. Both of them were despised by the onlookers who, like others (15v2), thought Jesus was wrong in going to the homes of such people. Jesus again explains that he is finding and saving people from being "lost", being away from the safety of friendship with God.
   • We don't know why it was so important to Jesus to spend time with Zacchaeus. He said that he <u>must</u> do it. The other things he had said he

<u>must</u> do were: be about his father's business (2v49); preach the good news of the Kingdom to other towns (4v43); suffer, be rejected, be killed, be raised to life (9v22); and keep going to Jerusalem (13v33). With such big things of his life being mentioned, we can see the importance of one person to Jesus when he adds to the list: staying overnight in Zacchaeus's home.

• Zacchaeus went out that day looking for Jesus, but from what Jesus did and said, it is clear that Jesus was looking for him, to bring him into a changed life.

Inspiring:

• The Holy Spirit was at work in Zacchaeus. He wanted to see Jesus, and was ready to welcome him.

• The Holy Spirit was at work with Jesus. Seeing Zacchaeus was an assignment Jesus had to fulfil, it was not a chance meeting. The Holy Spirit had somehow made Jesus aware of Zacchaeus's name, and of his readiness to accept Jesus.

• The Holy Spirit was at work in the outcome. Zacchaeus decided to give away half of what he had to the poor. This means that the poor blind beggar who had just been healed and had followed Jesus into Jericho would immediately have been provided for. This would have been a good start to his new life!

Instructing:

• There will be times when we will need to be determined (like Zacchaeus) and go after what we want in order to be in the place where Jesus will meet us.

• It is good to do what we can to put things right with people we have wronged, and to stop holding on to things that we should not have in our lives.

• We never know how near someone may be to giving their life to Jesus. Sometimes the most unexpected people (like Zacchaeus) are the ones who are most ready.

• When we are trying to help people to become Christians, we can be encouraged to know that Jesus is looking for them. He knows their name, and one experience of him could change them for ever.

74. 19v11-27 Jesus speaks about the coming Kingdom

Informing:

• People expected that if Jesus was the Messiah, he would go to Jerusalem and take over the government of Israel from the Romans by force.

• A mixture of people heard the parable. Some wanted to work for Jesus' Kingdom, some would have been content to do nothing about it, and some were against it. There were lessons that each could learn from the story.

• Jesus made use of things that had happened in that area as ideas in his story. To be made a king in that part of the Roman Empire, the person would have to go to Rome to be appointed. On one occasion people from Israel had sent a group of leaders to say to the Romans that they did not want the chosen man to be their king. (see - *Informing:* 85. 22v63-23v25)

• In this story, Jesus is talking about himself as the person being recognised as King.

• The money being given to each servant, a "mina", was worth about 100 days' wages.

• The story can be looked at in different ways:

1) Jesus "went away" when he died and then came back as king when he rose again and sent the Holy Spirit. His disciples then were given new responsibilities.

2) Jesus "went away" when he returned to heaven and we wait for him to come back some day to bring in God's Kingdom completely.

3) At different times in different places it can seem as if Jesus is "away" because there does not seem to be much of his Kingdom power being seen, and then times of "revival" come when the power of the Kingdom is seen and Christians who have been doing what they can in the "quiet" times are given greater work to do and the work of the enemy is pushed out.

Introducing:

• Like the man in the story, Jesus has received the right to be king. He did not have to fight for it, it already belonged to him.

161

• Like the man, Jesus will return and his Kingdom will come completely. We do not know when it will happen but we do know that it will happen.

• Like with the man, opposition does not stop Jesus being King.

• People who continue to oppose Jesus' Kingdom will eventually be removed. Until then they have the opportunity to change.

• The bad servant thought that the king wanted things done just for himself, but he was wrong. The king did not take the money earned; he let the good servants keep it! In the story the king was not agreeing that he was as the bad servant had described, but he was saying that if the servant was really afraid of him and thought of him as being mean and unfair, he could have at least put the money in the bank to get some interest. Jesus is very different from what people who oppose him think he is like. People use all sorts of excuses for not doing what they do not want to do.

Inspiring:

• The servants were given what they needed to trade with, and the Holy Spirit gives us what we need to do things that will help in the work of Jesus' Kingdom.

• Like the good servants recognised, the main reason that things increase in the work of Jesus' Kingdom is because of what he has given to us, not what we have done. The servants said, "Your money has earned this amount"; not (as in some Bibles) that they had earned it.

Instructing:

• We each have been given something to do which Jesus expects us to fulfil, whatever anyone else does. If we do not do it, then it may be given to someone else, and we will miss out on other things that we could have done for Jesus.

• When we do the littlest job well for Jesus, it can lead to us being given greater responsibility in his Kingdom, and we could suddenly be given a much bigger responsibility (like the first servant going from one gold coin to ten cities).

• Like the two good servants, we are different in our abilities. Jesus knows us very well. If he gives us something to do, we will be able to do it.

75. 19v28-40 Jesus approaches Jerusalem

Informing:
- Jerusalem was in hilly countryside. The village of Bethany was about two miles from Jerusalem.
- In the Old Testament, animals that were sacrificed were ones that had not been used for any work, and in that way they were set apart for God. The young donkey was like that in having never been ridden before.
- It is a common practice to lay a carpet down for an important person to enter. Those who placed clothes on the road were saying to Jesus and to everyone watching that Jesus was very special to them.
- The Pharisees in the crowd recognised Jesus as a teacher, but they did not consider themselves to be his followers. They told Jesus to rebuke those who were treating him as the Messiah, as the Pharisees did not believe him to be that. In replying that the stones would cry out, Jesus was saying that what was happening was completely what God wanted and that nothing would stop it.

Introducing:
- The Messiah coming into Jerusalem as King was part of Jesus' plan. He organised the getting of the donkey, allowed the people to place him on it, and went to enter Jerusalem in the way that had been prophesied hundreds of years before (Zechariah 9v9).
- Some people think that Jesus must have already arranged with the owners of the donkey for it to be available for his disciples to collect, but the account does not read that way, as the owners do not know why the disciples are taking it. It looks more as if the Holy Spirit had revealed the plan to Jesus, and he put it into action.
- Collecting the donkey was clearly an unusual thing to do, as the disciples were not to ask anyone for permission before taking it, but to give a simple explanation if asked why they had the right to take it. The word translated "owners" is the same word as is translated "Lord". So it is like saying that the people in charge asked them why they were taking the colt, and they answered that the person in charge needs it. Jesus is Lord over all, so if he needs a donkey (or anything else) he has the right to use it.

Inspiring:

• The Holy Spirit was at work in the finding and bringing of the donkey. The disciples found things just as Jesus had said.

• The Holy Spirit was at work in the crowd of Jesus' followers. They had been walking with him, when at some point, perhaps when Jerusalem came into view again, they burst into joyful praise. Those who had been on the journey had seen people healed of leprosy, the blind man being given back his sight, and Zacchaeus completely changed. Some would have begun on the journey with Jesus because they had already seen things he had done in another part of the country.

• The words of the crowd (v38) tell that these things have happened because King Jesus has power and authority given to him by God; because wholeness and blessing and peace have come to us from heaven; and because God's glory has come from the highest place and is seen in Jesus.

Instructing:

• If Jesus has instructed us to do something, we don't need to ask anyone's permission to do it, but we should be able to give a clear simple explanation of why we are doing what we are doing.

• We don't know if the two who were sent knew why Jesus wanted the donkey. Sometimes we may be given things to do that we do not fully understand. The Holy Spirit may give us information about what we can expect to happen when we do what he has told us.

• If, like the owners of the donkey, we have something which we hear that Jesus needs, we never know how important it might be in his plans.

• We might have expected Jesus to use a very experienced donkey for such an important job, especially with a lot of people around making a lot of noise. Even though, like the colt, we have no experience in something, we might be the very person that he chooses!

76. 19v41-48 Jesus comes into Jerusalem

Informing:
- The name "Jerusalem" means something like "Peace City".
- Jesus speaks about the <u>city</u> not being able to recognise and receive him. This is because even though many people there welcomed him, the leaders of the city made decisions which would affect the whole place, not only then, but in later years.
- About 30 years after this time the Jews became more and more unhappy because of the unfairness and cruelty of the Roman rulers. The Zealots, a group who believed that the way to deal with the situation was to use violence, led the Jews in an armed rebellion in AD66. The Jews won some victories and declared the independence of Israel. In April AD70, 60,000 Roman troops then surrounded Jerusalem which was full of people who had come for the Passover festival. In the following four months, thousands of people in the city died of starvation and disease, and many more died in the fighting which went on until the Romans destroyed the defences, killed the inhabitants and destroyed the temple. After another war in AD132, the Romans pulled down every building and built a new city on top of the ruins.
- People from other nations who were not Jews and who wanted to worship at the temple were allowed only into the outer courtyard which was also used for teaching. Animals were being sold there to be used in sacrifices, and money changers were charging people to exchange their money into the one kind of money that could be given at the temple. Doing these things in this courtyard got in the way of non-Jews worshipping and praying.
- The verse from Isaiah 56v7, which Jesus quotes part of, says that God's house would be a house of prayer <u>for</u> <u>all</u> <u>nations</u>.

Introducing:
- What changes of mood there are here! The crowd had been shouting with joy, and then suddenly Jesus is crying loudly in sadness about what is going to happen to Jerusalem. Later he is angry at what is happening in the temple courtyard, and then he is attracting many people with his

wonderful teaching.

• The things that Jesus says are going to happen do happen. In 9v22 Jesus said that he would be rejected by the Elders (leaders), Chief Priests and the Scribes (teachers of the law), and here we find that these are the people who are setting out to kill him. Also, what Jesus said here about what would happen to Jerusalem did happen.

Inspiring:

• The leaders in Jerusalem were not able to recognise what was happening because they had gone away from living God's way. When people accept wrong thoughts and they want things which are different from God's ways, they can miss when the Holy Spirit is at work very near them.

• The Holy Spirit sometimes gives people a vision of something that is going to happen in the future, like in Jesus knowing about Jerusalem. Sometimes we would like to know more than we do, but we should recognise that knowing more things from the Holy Spirit might mean that we would suffer the pain of sadness like Jesus did here. Let us be thankful for times when the Holy Spirit keeps things from us, as well as when he shows us special things.

Instructing:

• Keeping close to Jesus and learning from him is the way that we will be able to understand things clearly and recognise what God is doing. We don't want to miss it if he comes to our town in a special way.

• Times of rejoicing, times of feeling God's sadness, times of being angry when things are not right, and times of enjoying receiving from Jesus are all part of a life of following him.

• The Jews were so concerned to have things "right" for their worship at the temple that they put up notices to stop non-Jews going into their part of it, but they did not care about how buying and selling in the non-Jews area would affect the people who were trying to learn, worship and pray there. We should be careful when wanting our way of worship that we are not getting in the way of others worshipping.

77. 20v1-19 The leaders question Jesus

Informing:
• The Chief Priests, Teachers of the Law and the Elders considered themselves to be the people who had the authority to decide what was done or not done, and they were challenging Jesus because they had not given him the authority to do what he was doing, and so they wanted to stop him.

• Jesus' question to them about John the Baptist showed that they did not really care where authority came from; all they were concerned about was that they should be the ones in control.

• In the story, the owner of the vineyard is God, the vineyard is Israel (the nation through whom he had chosen to work in a special way), the workers were the leaders of Israel, the servants were the prophets that God had sent at various times in Israel's history and who had been rejected by the leaders. The loved son is Jesus.

The people who were listening understood what the story was about. Some parts of the Old Testament spoke of Israel as the Lord's vineyard (Isaiah 5v7). When they heard what could happen to it they were shocked because even though they knew that prophets had been rejected in the past, they could not believe that if God sent his son that he too would be rejected and that the leadership of those through whom God worked would be replaced.

• The leaders of that time, who were listening, knew that he was speaking about them.

Introducing:
• The Good News that Jesus is bringing in his teaching (v1) is the Good News of God's Kingdom. He is telling and showing the good things that happen when life is governed by what God wants, so he is speaking about God's authority.

• Jesus speaks of himself in the parable as the "loved son". This is the same description spoken of him at his baptism (3v22) and on the mountain (9v35).

• Though the crowd could not believe that God's special one would be rejected, Jesus showed that this fitted with what had been prophesied in Psalm 118v22, the same psalm that they had quoted when they had shouted their welcome to him as he came into Jerusalem (19v38).

• Jesus describes himself as the stone which holds a building together. He then says that he is a stone which is not only important, it is also very strong. Anything that hits against it is not going to break it; anything that it hits is going to be crushed. So when people try to use their power against Jesus, they are going to be defeated, and when Jesus uses his power, he is powerful enough to win completely. In Daniel 2v44,45 the picture is used of God setting up a kingdom which cannot be destroyed like a stone which breaks in pieces iron, brass, clay, silver and gold (other kingdoms), so Jesus is using ideas that the listeners would have understood.

Inspiring:

• The parable, which illustrates God's dealings with Israel in its history, shows the patience of God in dealing with his people and those to whom he has given responsibility. When God holds back from intervening, people can think that he never will and that they can do what they like. But there does come the time when God steps in to change things. Those who resist the Holy Spirit never win, although they may appear to have some authority for a time.

Instructing:

• When we live for Jesus and do what he wants, there will be times when people question our right to be doing what we are doing. This can come particularly from people involved in Christian things who believe that they should be in control of what others are doing. We should look for the right Holy Spirit answer to give them, and recognise that whatever we say, it may not change their minds. So, like Jesus, we should make sure that we don't stop talking to the others who want to listen.

• The crowd quoted one part of a psalm and missed the other part which Jesus then told them about. When we are using the Bible, we should be careful when we use particular verses that we do not avoid other ones which we do not find so attractive.

78. 20v20-26 Jesus answers an awkward question

Informing:

• The Jewish leaders, afraid of the crowd turning against them if they took action against Jesus, planned to try to get him to do something which was not just breaking Jewish laws, but breaking Roman laws. This would mean that the Roman rulers would have to deal with him. The Romans allowed the Jewish leaders to have a certain amount of authority to deal with their own people, but the Roman governor was the only one who could sentence someone to death.

• The question that was asked was a clever one. If Jesus said that it was lawful for Jews to pay taxes to Caesar, the Roman emperor, then the crowd of people following him might have been disappointed. It would look as if Jesus was accepting the Roman government of Israel as right, when they considered it to be something to be changed, and they expected the Messiah to change it! If Jesus said that it was not lawful, then that would be enough evidence for the Jewish leaders to take to the Roman authorities to accuse Jesus of wrongdoing.

Introducing:

• The description of Jesus in v21, although given by people who did not believe it to be true, is a very good description of him. He did say whatever was right and true, whoever he was talking to.

• Jesus was very good at answering awkward questions. Here, the questioners, pretending to be honest, very religious people, probably expected Jesus to say something like, "No, our law requires that we keep ourselves completely clean from contact with people who don't believe in God and who break his commandments by making images of their emperor on their coins." (This would have been the view of some Jews). Jesus asked them to show him a coin, and since they had one with the Roman emperor's head on it, this showed that they themselves had dealings with the Romans as they were using Roman money.

• It can be taken from what Jesus said that it is right to pay taxes, as the government is responsible for managing the country and has a right to be given money to do that.

But also, when Jesus said to pay to Caesar what is Caesar's, he did not say exactly what things do belong to Caesar, and by saying to pay to God what belongs to God, he shows that anything that Caesar (or anyone else) demands which is against what God requires does not have to be given.

Inspiring:
• People's words do not always show what is going on in their hearts. The Holy Spirit can give us discernment, the ability to recognise why people are saying what they are saying.

• The Holy Spirit can give us the right answer when we are faced with difficult questions.

• If what belongs to Caesar is the thing that he has made with his image on it (the coins), then what belongs to God is what he has made with <u>his</u> image on it. That is us - people (Genesis 1v26). So giving to God what belongs to him means giving our whole lives to him.

Instructing:
• When we are living for Jesus there will sometimes be people around us who will be watching what we are doing and saying in order to catch us out.

• While not being afraid to say and do what is right, whoever we are talking to, we should be careful in answering questions. There will be times when we think we know the right answer, but we should ask the Holy Spirit for wisdom in saying the right thing for that situation and person.

• We should be careful when people that we do not know say nice things to us. While they may be genuine, their words may be a way of making us feel safe so that we then say things to them that we should not. It is good to ask the Holy Spirit to give us discernment for all such conversations.

---

79. 20v27-47 Sadducees ask about life after death

Informing:
• The Sadducees were a particular group of Jews, mainly powerful priestly families. Unlike the Pharisees, they had the belief that only the "Books of Moses" (Genesis, Exodus, Leviticus, Numbers and Deuteronomy) should be accepted as having authority, and they rejected teachings that they thought came after that time including belief in resurrection (life after death), angels or spirits.

• The Sadducees are not looking to learn from Jesus. They are trying to make fun of him by what they think is an argument which shows that belief in a life after death cannot fit with Moses' teaching.

• The instruction of Moses (Deuteronomy 25v5) was a way of someone honouring his brother by marrying his widow and having a child who would continue that family.

Introducing:
• Jesus shows where they are wrong in their beliefs. They think that believing in resurrection means believing in a life after death which is the same as life before death. Jesus speaks of life after death as another age which is different to the time we now live in, and of a different order. Saying that there will be no marriage does not mean that life in that age will be any less in joy and fulfilment. Whoever God brings into undying life with him (like the angels enjoy), will all be his children, his family.

• Jesus speaks of having to be counted as worthy in order to enter into the enjoyment of resurrection life. He points out that those who are not worthy (like the proud Teachers of the Law who have misused their position) will face very severe punishment in that next age.

• Since the Sadducees base their beliefs on the writings of Moses, Jesus uses Moses' writings to show that there is life after death. When God spoke to Moses at the burning bush (Exodus 3v6) he said that he is the God of ancestors of Moses who had died a long time before, showing that they must still be alive (with God in heaven).

• It is not surprising that one of the Teachers of the Law liked Jesus' answer, as they (along with the Pharisees) disagreed with the Sadducees and thought that they themselves were right in everything to do with understanding the Old Testament. But Jesus challenges their thinking too. They were looking for a descendant of King David to be the Messiah. What David said about God speaking to his Lord (the Messiah) would mean that the Messiah was already living in David's time or before. Jesus, by asking the question, is showing them that there are things that they do not understand fully. Jesus is saying that he is more than just a man like others; he had a heavenly life before he was born as a human baby. So the Teachers of the Law who had been happy to agree with Jesus about life after death are being made to think about whether they believe in the Messiah's life before birth.

Inspiring:

- Some people wrongly decide to not accept the authority of parts of the Bible.
- Some people say they don't believe in something "because it's not in the Bible", when if they looked more closely they would find it.
- Some people argue about things in the Bible when they don't understand what it is saying.
- Some people say that they base what they do and say on what is written in the Bible but their teaching and actions are very different from what Jesus showed to be true.
- We need the Holy Spirit to give us understanding of the Bible, and to help us grow in our understanding.

Instructing:

- It is important for us to grow in our knowledge of the Bible, and to recognise that we don't understand everything. We should be careful when we see where others are wrong in their thinking that we do not think that we know everything. Let us be very thankful for all that the Holy Spirit has shown us so far, and continue as humble learners, taking care not to become arrogant, and not to go along with people who are.

80. 21v1-4 Jesus notices a special offering

Informing:

• In one of the courtyards of the temple there were 13 trumpet shaped containers into which people could put their gifts as part of their worship. Each container was labelled for the particular thing that the money placed there would be used for.

• The word used about the rich people giving means that they were giving from what was left over after they had used all they needed for themselves.

• The word describing the widow as poor in verse 2 suggests that she had to work for her own support. She was not a beggar. So after giving her gift, she would have had to go and work before having anything else for herself.

• The woman had suffered the death of her husband and had very little, but she did not let that get in the way of her worshipping God. We do not know how far she had come, or how often she was able to visit the temple, but she took this opportunity to give what she could.

• The coins that she gave were the smallest coins in Jewish money.

Introducing:

• Jesus notices what other people might miss. He notices the widow giving.

• Jesus sees things in a different way from other people. Others saw how little her gift was; Jesus saw how much it was costing her.

• Jesus knows things that other people do not know. Others knew that she gave two small coins; Jesus knew that she was giving all the money she had.

Inspiring:

• Jesus may have seen by her dress that the woman was a widow and that she was poor, but he would have known that she was giving all she had by the Holy Spirit revealing that to him.

• The Holy Spirit can use the little we have to give, in ways that are beyond what we can see or know. The two coins themselves would not make much difference to anything, but her giving of them has been used by the Holy Spirit ever since that time to speak to everyone who has read Luke's book, even now giving us an example for our own worship and our giving to God.

• Just as Jesus was watching the widow, so the Holy Spirit watches us and sees what we are doing. He knows and appreciates when we do not have much that we can give, and when living for Jesus is costing us more than others will ever know.

Instructing:

• Some people might have said that it was not sensible or needed for the widow to give in such a way which would leave her with nothing at that time. There may be times for us when what we do for Jesus is not thought of by others as needed or sensible, while to us it becomes an adventure of trusting Jesus more.

• The widow's example should challenge us about how much we give away for the work of Jesus' Kingdom.

• We should not be discouraged if we feel that we do not have much to give. Small gifts can be very important to Jesus.

• Let us grow in seeing and noticing things in the way that Jesus did, so that rather than being impressed by the things that impress others (like the big gifts of rich people), we recognise the big love and worship that may be being given by someone whom others do not think important.

• When Jesus mentioned the widow's situation to the people around him, I wonder whether any of them then went to offer some help to her. When Jesus brings some need to our attention, it may be that he wants us to do something about it. We should ask him.

81. 21v5-36 Jesus talks about the future

Informing:
• Jesus speaks of things that will happen to those he is talking to at the time, like in verses 12-16, and these things did happen in that way (for example in Acts 4v3-14).

• Jesus speaks of the destruction of Jerusalem (v20-24), and in AD70 it happened. Christians at that time did leave the city and so escaped before it happened.

• Jesus speaks of things that would happen until the time when he would return in power (v8-11). These things have been happening in different ways ever since.

• Jesus speaks of things that will happen just before his return in power (v25-26), and they will happen too, just as Jesus said that they would.

• When Jesus says in verse 18 that not even a hair of your head will perish, he does not mean that his followers will not suffer. He has just said that some will be killed for following him. He means that they will come through death into new life complete, without having been made any the less by any hardships they have been through.

• When Jesus says in verse 32 that this generation will not pass away until all has happened, he cannot mean that all the things he had spoken of would happen while that group of people was still alive, since there are parts of what he said that are still to happen. We cannot say for certain what Jesus meant by these words. It could be read as speaking about the part that they had asked about, that is about the temple and Jerusalem. It may mean that it would all begin to happen at that time, and that what is happening now in the world is all part of the same ongoing time. It could mean that when "the end times" come as described from verse 25, those things will all happen in one generation (about 30- 40 years). Whenever the phrase "this generation" is used in Luke's book it is speaking not just about people who were alive at that time, but about the kind of people who were rejecting God's ways, so Jesus may have meant that instead of everyone gradually accepting him and following God's ways (which is what the disciples might have hoped for), there would be, right to the end, the same sort of people who opposed God's ways.

175

Introducing:

• Jesus is making it clear that there will be a long time between Jesus being with his disciples and when he returns to bring God's Kingdom in fully.

• While we do not know the exact times of all the different things that Jesus speaks about, it is clear that everything in the world is going to change when Jesus returns and his greatness and power is known by everyone.

• Much of what Jesus is saying is to encourage his followers, then and now, to keep living in his way so that whatever happens they will come through all these things to stand before him, which is to meet him without guilt or shame or fear. Jesus is looking forward to meeting us!

Inspiring:

• In verse 15, Jesus promises that <u>he</u> will give his disciples what they need when they are questioned. But he would not be there at that time, so how will he give to them? The answer is in 12v12 where Jesus had said that <u>the Holy Spirit </u>would teach them at the time what to say.

• The Holy Spirit can show what is true about what people are saying. (v8)

• The Holy Spirit can give us the right words to say. (v15)

• The Holy Spirit can give us peace through difficult times. (v19)

• The Holy Spirit can tell us what to do in difficult situations. (v21)

Instructing:

• Don't be tricked (by people who claim something special). (v8)

• Don't be scared (by bad things happening in the world). (v9)

• Don't worry about what to say (when asked difficult questions). (v14)

• Don't lose your peace (when people reject you). (v19)

• Don't ignore God's signs (when he tells you what to do). (v20, 21)

• Don't lose hope (when frightening things are happening). (v28)

• Don't lose your focus on what is important (when things take longer than you expect). (v34)

• Don't stop asking God for all you need (whatever you are going through). (v36)

82. 21v37-22v23 Jesus arranges a special meal

Informing:

• More than a thousand years before this time, when the Israelites were slaves in Egypt, God instructed Moses to lead them out to freedom. The ruler of Egypt would not allow them to go. God sent plagues as warnings to do as he said. The ruler, Pharaoh was very stubborn, so God warned that he would kill all the oldest members of each family in the land during one night. The Israelites were to kill a lamb for each house and sprinkle its blood on the doorposts as a sign that they belonged to God and so would escape the judgement. So God's judgement "passed over" them. The lamb was then roasted and eaten at a special meal. From then on, the Israelites celebrated a yearly Passover meal followed by a festival week when they ate unleavened bread (flat bread without yeast in it), as a reminder of God taking them so quickly out of Egypt that they did not have time to make normal bread which needs more time for the dough to rise. (See Exodus 12)

• Luke does not give any more information about what led up to Judas betraying Jesus. In John 12v6 it mentions that Judas took money for himself which was not his. By having his heart set on things that were wrong, Judas opened a door in his life that Satan was able to come through and take over.

• Satan – see *Informing:* 14. 4v1-15.

Introducing:

• Ordinary people loved hearing Jesus and being with him. It was the religious authorities who hated him.

• Just as Jesus had taken part in being baptised by John as a way of beginning his new mission, here he takes part in the Passover as a way of bringing in the new way of God's dealings with his people. Instead of focussing on remembering God taking his people quickly out of slavery in Egypt, his followers are to focus on God setting them free from sin by what Jesus is about to do in the next day. Instead of God marking out who his people were by those who associated with the blood of a lamb, they were to understand God now marking out who were his people by those who associate with the blood of Jesus in his death for them.

• Jesus speaks of the blood of the new covenant or new testament. We think of the New Testament as a book, a part of the Bible, but it means the New Agreement that God has made in how he will deal with us now that Jesus has done all that is needed to make us right with God.

• When Jesus had spoken before about the Kingdom of God, he had spoken about waiting times, but here he is making it clear that some special events in God's Kingdom were about to happen quickly, before he would eat and drink again.

• In verse 22, Jesus shows that while his suffering and death involved the evil plans of people like Judas, those plans would be used to bring about a much greater plan that God had decided.

Inspiring:

• When Jesus sent Peter and John, how did he know that there would be a man carrying a water jar? How did he know they would get to the right place at the minute the man would walk past? The Holy Spirit can give information, direction and timing for things to work out as God wants.

Instructing:

• We do not know what arrangements (if any) Jesus had previously made with the owner of the house he sent Peter and John to. When, like them, we follow the instructions that Jesus has given us (not knowing how it can all work out), we will find that it will fit with arrangements he has prepared with people and places that we do not know.

• It is sadly true that from time to time it happens that someone who has appeared to be following Jesus is found to be living in a way that is completely against Jesus' ways. We might think, "How did I not see that they were like that?", but it could be, that for whatever reason, Jesus decided not to let us know about it, in the same way that although he knew about Judas, Jesus did not tell the other disciples about him.

83. 22v24-38 Disciples argue about being great

Informing:

• Jesus, in saying that the disciples would eat at his table, shows that they would have a place of great honour alongside him.

• The disciples would have understood the twelve tribes of Israel to mean all God's people. The tribes were the families of the twelve sons of Jacob whose name was changed by God to Israel. Judging them would not mean being like a judge in a court, but rather making leadership decisions affecting them.

• While the disciples had been looking for a special place, each for himself, Jesus promises them a special place for all of them, not one above the others.

• When Jesus said that Peter would deny him before the cock crows "today", that was because days were marked from sunset to sunset, rather than from midnight to midnight.

• What Jesus says about selling cloaks to buy swords is clearly "picture language". He did not expect them to fight with swords, and the opposition they were about to face was going to happen in the next few hours. He was telling them to be prepared for a difficult time. That is why he said, "That's enough" when they mentioned they had two swords, not that two swords would be enough for them to fight with.

Introducing:

• Jesus teaches here how his Kingdom works. It is not like the ways in which other kingdoms, nations or governments work. In them, the leaders decide what people can and cannot do, and it is thought that they are good leaders if they can get people to do what they want them to do. In Jesus' Kingdom, good leaders behave like the youngest, that is in respecting others and expecting that others may have more wisdom than they have. Instead of looking to get people to obey and do things for them, they will see what others need and try to provide it, as Jesus did.

• When Jesus said that what was written about him was about to happen, the words he spoke were from Isaiah 53v12. That whole chapter, written about 700 years before, describes what Jesus would suffer to fulfil

God's plan.

• Jesus wants his followers to keep trusting him. They have trusted him enough to stay with him; they can trust him for a special place in his Kingdom. They have trusted him on missions; they are now to trust him in times of opposition. Peter will soon say that he is not with Jesus; Jesus does not want that experience to stop Peter trusting him. Although <u>Peter</u> would fail, Jesus prayed that his <u>faith</u> would not fail.

Inspiring:

• Satan wanted to sift the disciples, that is, to shake them, like things of different sizes going through a sieve. He hoped to find weaknesses in some of them to separate them and take them for himself. The Holy Spirit knew his plans. While Peter might have thought of himself as the strongest, Jesus knew that he was the most likely to fail, so he singles him out for a special Holy Spirit warning of what is about to happen, and the assurance that he will come through it to be able to set the direction for the other followers of Jesus. Sometimes the Holy Spirit does not prevent us going through Satan's attacks, but uses them to bring us through to being stronger in our experience of Jesus.

• There will be times when the Holy Spirit will warn us of things that are about to happen in order for us to be prepared, and for us to help others to be prepared to trust Jesus through difficult times.

Instructing:

• If we want to give a lead to others, we should do it by being like their servants, to provide what they need. That is not the thing to do so that you can <u>become</u> a leader; it is the thing to do because you <u>are</u> a leader.

• There will be times when we are well received, like the disciples had been on their missions, and other times when we will face opposition and rejection, like Jesus was warning them about. We should be ready to follow different instructions from Jesus in these different times. It is important to listen to what he wants us to do today, not just to follow what he said to us at a different time in a different situation.

• There are times when because of our weakness, we fail to be all that we should be as followers of Jesus. What Jesus wants for us at times like that, is that we do not allow our sense of failure to stop us trusting him, but that we look for his help and friendship again. He still has great plans for us.

84. 22v39-62 Jesus prays and is then arrested

Informing:
- The Mount of Olives (21v37) was where Jesus and the disciples had spent each night that week.
- Jesus describes what he is about to face as being like a cup that his Father is giving him to drink. Where this picture is used in the Old Testament it speaks of a cup full of God's anger against sin.
- Although the disciples fell asleep while Jesus was praying, some of them must have been awake long enough to hear what he prayed and to see the struggle he was going through.
- Jesus was so stressed that sweat was pouring from him as if he was bleeding. In extreme stress it is possible for blood vessels to burst so there may have been blood in his sweat.
- The crowd was made up of the religious leaders and people they had brought.
- A kiss, normally a greeting of friendship, was the sign that Judas had arranged to show which one was Jesus.
- Darkness was the cover that they used to arrest Jesus without anyone else seeing. This too was the time when "darkness" (the force of evil) was going to be allowed to do its worst against Jesus.

Introducing:
- Jesus here is experiencing the most awesome struggle. He knows what he is about to face and can see the pain that it is going to mean for him. He is praying that if possible he might not have to go through with it, but he agrees with his Father's plan. It was his Father's decision to "give him the cup"; it was Jesus' decision to choose to "drink it".
- When Jesus got up from praying, he had settled that he was accepting what was to come, and there was from that time a calmness in him as he went on from there.
- In the middle of Jesus facing the most awful pain and suffering, he is still thinking of others. He tells the disciples to pray for strength for themselves, he heals the man whose ear was cut off, and he looks round at Peter.

Inspiring:
• Prayer brings us the Holy Spirit resources we need to face difficult times. The angel sent to Jesus was not to make his pain less, but to enable him to endure even more pain.

• We do not have the strength on our own to face testing times. We need the strength that the Holy Spirit can give us, otherwise we may enter or fall into temptation, that is, make a decision which takes us out of what God wants for us.

Instructing:
• While our lives should be full of prayer, special times of crisis should lead us to special times of prayer, asking either to escape from the situation, or if not, then to endure and come through the situation with strength from heaven.

• At such times it may not be easy to pray. Tiredness, depression and grief may get in our way, but resources from Jesus are available to us if we ask for them.

• It is important that when we ask Jesus for something, we wait for an answer, not like the disciple who didn't wait for an answer about using the sword. He went ahead and did something which may have seemed right to him, but was not what Jesus wanted.

• When Peter was not expecting it, he was recognised as one of Jesus' disciples. People take a lot more notice than we realise of how we live as Christians. They especially notice when we do something that we should not be doing!

• At any time when we are ashamed of what we have done, when we are disappointed at ourselves, we should remember that Jesus knows us better than we know ourselves, he still loves us, and we can turn back to him.

85. 22v63-23v25 Jesus is put on trial

Informing:

• The Council (known as the Sanhedrin) was allowed by the Roman government to decide matters for the Jewish people about religious and criminal wrongdoing. Anything that required the death penalty had to be passed to the Roman governor, Pilate for his decision.

• The Council had rules for conducting trials, but these were all set aside in their rush to get Jesus condemned before the ordinary people would know what they were trying to do.

• The Council decided that Jesus was guilty of insulting God and so deserved the death penalty. They knew Pilate would not condemn him to death for a religious wrongdoing, so that is why they tried to invent evidence to accuse him of stirring up rebellion against the Romans.

• Leading up to the time when Jesus was born, there had been a Herod who the Romans allowed to be the ruler of land including Galilee and Judea. The Romans gave him the title, "King of the Jews". He left his kingdom to his three sons. The Herod who was given Judea was so bad that the Jewish leaders went to Rome and asked them to remove him. The Romans took over the government of that area and appointed Pilate. The Herod who was given Galilee had killed John the Baptist and is the one mentioned here. So for Jesus to be "King of the Jews" would be seen by Pilate and Herod as taking their place. They did not see him as a serious dangerous threat, but as a weak person to be made fun of.

• Each year, at the time of this feast, Pilate released a prisoner, so he was suggesting that Jesus could be the one to be released that day.

• Crucifixion was a cruel way of executing criminals that the Romans used. There were different ways it was done involving nailing the person's hands and feet to a cross of wood which was stood upright in the ground. They were left to hang there until they died.

Introducing:

• When Jesus spoke of the Son of Man being at the right hand of God, it would have been taken as referring to the words in Psalm 110v1, which Jesus quoted in 20v42 and which were about the place of the Messiah.

That is why they then asked him if he was saying he was that person, the Son of God.

• Because Jesus did not resist what was being done to him, the people who were abusing him thought that he was weak, when instead he was being meek, that is deliberately holding back from what he could have chosen to do and say.

Inspiring:

• When people deliberately reject the Holy Spirit, like the Jewish leaders were doing by opposing Jesus, it opens the way for them to be influenced by all sorts of evil. Those who had the position of leading God's people had instead become enemies of God's Kingdom.

• The Holy Spirit can still bring about God's plans even when it looks as if everything is against him. He was doing that here, though no one but Jesus understood at the time.

Instructing:

• Sometimes it is right to stay quiet (as Jesus did with Herod) and not to answer the questions that people are asking, when they are only interested in attacking us. The Holy Spirit can give us the right words, or the right silence.

• We may come across people like those in this passage:

1) The guards who take advantage of someone who appears to be weak.

2) Pilate who knows what is right, but chooses to agree to what the crowd wants.

3) The religious leaders who have a show of being godly, but are opposed to God.

4) Herod who wants to see Jesus but with no intention of having his life changed.

5) The followers of the religious leaders who shout for someone to be crucified when he has done nothing wrong.

• May the Holy Spirit keep us from being like any of them, and give us wisdom when we meet people like them.

86. 23v26-48 Jesus is crucified

Informing:
• Cyrene where Simon came from was in North Africa, more than 800 miles from Jerusalem. Mark says (Mark 15v21) that Simon is the father of Alexander and Rufus. They must have been known to the Christians he was writing to.

• Usually, the person being crucified carried his own cross. It looks as if Jesus had been so badly beaten by this time that he was not able to do so.

• The crowd watching would have been a mix of those who had called for his death, and a large number of others who every day that week had come early each morning to hear him (21v38).

• Roman soldiers carried out the crucifixion. The centurion was the officer in charge.

• In speaking to the women, Jesus was prophesying the time when Jerusalem would be besieged and destroyed. This was going to be so awful that people would want a quick death (like mountains falling on them) rather than the long slow suffering that they would experience. (see *Informing: 76. 19v41-48*)

• The crime of the person being crucified was written on a board. Greek was the well-known international language at that time, Latin was the language of the Romans, and Hebrew was the language of the Jews.

• The Romans did not write that Jesus was rebelling against the government as the chief priests had said. In putting "the King of the Jews", the Romans were having a joke against the Jews with the idea that they had asked this foreign government to kill their own king.

Introducing:
• In this time of great suffering, Jesus cares about those who are friendly to him, the grieving women. He also cares about those who are crucifying him. His prayer for forgiveness especially applied to the soldiers who were simply doing what they had been ordered to do.

• Paradise was the name given to large gardens with trees that kings had for their enjoyment. So when the criminal recognised Jesus as his king and knew that at some time after death Jesus would be in his kingdom,

185

Jesus promise to him is like, "Later on today, you and I will go for a walk together in my royal park."

• Jesus, when he had done everything, was able to die at the time he chose. When he had said he was giving his spirit to his Father, it happened.

Inspiring:

• A tree would be green when there was water, and dry when there was no water. When Jesus was in Jerusalem there had been lots of Holy Spirit "water" with him, yet the leaders were making evil decisions. How much worse they would be he was no longer there.

• The Holy Spirit's power can change a person in a very short time, like when the criminal came to know the truth about Jesus and put his trust in him.

• The Holy Spirit works through unusual things happening at a particular time. Darkness came across the sky for three hours in the middle of the day, and then it became light again when Jesus died. The curtain in the temple which covered the most holy place was torn in two. Seeing the things that happened when Jesus was on the cross, made <u>everyone</u> who had come to watch realise that something awful had happened.

Instructing:

• God's coincidences can place us in the right place to come into closeness with Jesus even when the situation we face may be surprising or even shocking. That happened here for Simon, the grieving women, the criminal, and the centurion.

• We can look for what the Holy Spirit is doing, knowing that Jesus always has a plan he is working to, whatever others are doing.

• In the temple, only the high priest, once a year was allowed to go behind the curtain into the most holy place with blood from an animal sacrifice offered for the people's wrongdoing. The curtain was a picture of us not being able to come into God's presence because of our sin. The curtain being torn apart showed that the sacrifice of Jesus dealt completely with sin (see Hebrews 9v26), so the curtain is no longer needed, and we can come with confidence to God because of what Jesus has done. Jesus' death brings to an end the need for animal sacrifices in worship.

87. 23v49-24v12 Friends come to Jesus' tomb

Informing:
- The women from Galilee, including Mary Magdalene and Joanna, are described in *Informing:* 34. 8v1-3
- Joseph was one of the leadership council which had decided to have Jesus put to death, but he had not agreed with that decision.
- Taking Jesus' body down from the cross was a messy unpleasant job. Joseph was helped in this by another council member, Nicodemus (John19v39).
- The tomb was like a small room cut out of rock. The stone to cover the entrance would have been shaped like a wheel, and rolled into place along a groove.
- The day before the Sabbath was the Preparation day to get things ready so that no work would have to be done during the Sabbath.
- The spices and perfumes that the women were preparing were for anointing the dead body.

Introducing:
- In Isaiah 53v9, it says that the Lord's Servant would be associated with criminals and the rich in his death. Jesus was crucified between two criminals, and was laid in the tomb of a rich man, Joseph.
- Jesus had not just passed through death to be alive in heaven; he had taken up life again in his body. Those whom Jesus had brought back to life lived the rest of their lives in a "healed" body, but then died naturally later. In contrast to that, Jesus' body was changed to be no longer limited in the way that our bodies are.
- The grave-clothes still lying in the tomb showed that something extraordinary had happened to the body. It also showed that no one had removed the body, because if they had, they would not have unwrapped it before taking it away.

Inspiring:
- The Holy Spirit is able to arrange for someone to be just right for a particular thing that needs to be done. Joseph of Arimathea was able to

do what the disciples and the women were not able to do. Sometimes, we will be the person who has been prepared by the Holy Spirit for some work that others are not able to do.

• One part of the Holy Spirit's work is to remind us of what Jesus has said and done. Here two angels help in making sure that the women get the message!

• There may be times when it seems that nothing is as it should be, like Joseph experienced when Jesus was crucified. At such a time, the Holy Spirit may have something special for us to do in preparation for what is to come.

Instructing:

• If we take care to get to know and understand Jesus' words, we will be less often in situations where we do not understand what is happening.

• There are times when it seems that there is nothing we can do, like it was for those who knew Jesus and were looking on at a distance. God will have a plan, like he had on that occasion when they then saw an unlikely person, a member of the council, come to take care of things.

• The spices that the women had prepared were not needed. Sometimes we prepare something as an offering to Jesus which is not used. However, such expressions of love and worship are not wasted. Bringing them, we can find ourselves, like the women did, in just the right place for something even more special than we were expecting.

• If God gives us special experiences, we would think that others would be helped by us telling them. Sometimes, like the women found, even though our experience is very real to us, others have difficulty in receiving what we say.

• We find it difficult to believe things that we have not experienced before. Whenever there are times of revival, there are Christians who oppose what is happening because it is different from what has been in their experience. If we hear of things happening that sound like "nonsense" to us, we should perhaps follow Peter's example here, and investigate and think about things for ourselves. There may be something wonderful about Jesus for us to discover in what is happening.

88. 24v13-35 Two friends walk and talk with Jesus

Informing:
• Jesus' work involves not just well known people, but also the unknown, like Cleopas, the other person with him (we are not told anything more about them), and those in the group of people with the apostles who were together that evening in Jerusalem.

• It looks as if these two had decided that whatever was going to happen had happened, and that there was nothing more for them to wait for in Jerusalem. So unlike others who were staying together, they set off for home.

• Their conversation was loud enough for Jesus to hear them discussing, and his question to them uses a word which means they were throwing words to each other.

• They were kept from recognising Jesus because there was a particular way that he wanted to use the time with them.

• When they did recognise him, I wonder whether it happened by them seeing his hands when he broke the bread and handed it to them. His hands had the marks that the nails made in them.

• They walked a long way that day, as having just walked about seven miles from Jerusalem to Emmaus, they then walked (or maybe ran?) all the way back!

Introducing:
• There is something of fun and enjoyment in the way that Jesus related to these two as if he does not know them. I imagine a smile on his face when they ask him if he is the only one who does not know what has been happening! Then after maybe three or four hours, at the point when they suddenly realise who he is, he disappears. When they get back to Jerusalem he will have another surprise for them.

• In talking to them without them knowing who he was, Jesus taught them to understand his suffering and his death first so that they would then fully understand his rising from death.

• Jesus' conversation showed that <u>all</u> of the Old Testament writings speak in some way about him. A clear purpose of those books is to help us to know Jesus better.

• We see here some things about Jesus' "risen from the dead body". He looked like an ordinary person. He was able to be not recognised by people who knew him. He could disappear from sight.

Inspiring:

• The key to understanding what is happening is knowing what is in the Bible, and the key to understanding what is in the Bible is knowing that it all speaks of Jesus. The Holy Spirit, who inspired the words in the Bible to be written in the way they were, is also the one who can give us understanding of their meaning.

• Sometimes the Holy Spirit will keep us from seeing something, like when the two did not recognise Jesus. As at that time, Jesus may have something particular to teach us, before he leads us into a new experience.

Instructing:

• When we think that there may be nothing more to wait for, we may be just about to discover much more of what Jesus has to say and do in our lives.

• Jesus said that they were slow to believe all that the prophets have spoken. They had accepted the parts about the victory of the Messiah, but not the parts about his suffering. We should be careful not to just believe and accept the parts of the Bible that we like.

• Jesus went into their house because they made it very clear that they wanted him to stay with them. Sometimes Jesus may give us the opportunity to receive more from him and he will wait for us to ask him.

• Although there was the amazing miracle of Jesus disappearing from their sight, the thing that the two recognised as important was the fiery inner excitement they had when Jesus talked with them. One of the most amazing things for us is to hear Jesus speak to us through the words in the Bible.

• Jesus had appeared at some time that day to Simon Peter. We are not told anything more about that meeting. Some of our experiences of Jesus are for sharing; others, like Peter's meeting, are not meant to be talked about.

89. 24v36-53 Jesus surprises his disciples

Informing:
• There is some fun in the way that the two from Emmaus hurry back to tell the others that Jesus is alive, only to find when they get there, that they already know; and before they can finish their story of Jesus disappearing from them, he suddenly appears in the middle of the crowded room!

• Luke here gives just a short account of what happened between Jesus rising from the dead and then going to heaven. In his second book (Acts 1v1-11) he gives more details of those 40 days. For some of that time, Jesus' disciples were in Galilee and Jesus appeared to them there (Matthew 28v7,16; John 21). At one time Jesus appeared to more than 500 of his followers at the same time (1 Corinthians 15v6).

• The beginning of Luke's book has the promise of Good News of great joy for all the people (2v10). The end of Luke's book has great joy in those who are about to take the Good News to every nation.

Introducing:
• Since his sudden appearance was a bit of a shock, Jesus makes it clear that they really are seeing <u>him</u>, nothing less. His hands and feet would have shown the marks of the nails. Touching him and feeling him showed that he was not just something they were seeing in their minds. This would be important later when people would want to know how they knew that it was really him. By eating with them Jesus showed that he was no less than he had always been, a real person, but not now limited in the ways that normal people are.

• Jesus, in explaining the Scriptures about himself, showed that everything that had happened to him was according to God's plan. Different parts of that plan had been written about in all the parts of the Old Testament. Jesus' dying and rising from death are not the end of God's plan, but the centre of it. From that time God's plan continues in bringing his message to people of every nation. Because of what Jesus has done, when people are willing to turn from wrong and are ready to do what God wants, then their sin, their failure is "sent away", forgiven.

Inspiring:

• The Holy Spirit opens our minds to understand things. When we can see (as Jesus showed) that part of God's plan was for his chosen Messiah to suffer and die, we can then understand the parts of the Bible that speak about that. If we did not know about that plan, we would not be able to understand what those passages were about.

• The Holy Spirit is what Jesus' Father promised, and the words used describe his coming as being like his followers putting on power-clothes from heaven. More is said about this in Acts 1, and the coming of the Holy Spirit to them is written about in Acts 2.

Instructing:

• Witnesses speak not just about things they <u>believe</u> to be true, but of something which they <u>know</u> to be true because they have seen and experienced it. This is what Jesus' disciples are to do, then and now.

• Although the people were talking to each other about knowing that Jesus was alive, they were then shocked to see him. They still needed to be convinced that it really was him! What we know to be true about Jesus should make us ready for whatever he may do, and we should not be surprised to see his power is in action.

• We each have some part in God's ongoing plan for the Good News about Jesus to go to people of every nation by the Holy Spirit working through us. We will know the part that we have in the same way that Jesus' followers knew then, by listening to Jesus speaking to us by the Holy Spirit and through the Bible. We cannot do it in our own strength, or in the time that we choose. Just like Jesus told the disciples, he has the right time, the right place and the right power for us to do what he wants us to do. Sometimes the hardest thing to do is to have to sit and wait as they had to. In the meantime, we can do as they did – worship Jesus with joy together, looking for whatever is next in the wonderful adventure of living for him.

Lightning Source UK Ltd.
Milton Keynes UK
UKOW030057301011

181157UK00001B/6/P